Mapping the Hero's Journey With Tarot:

33 Days to Finish Your Book

Arwen Lynch

Mapping The Hero's Journey, Copyright 2017, Arwen Lynch-Poe
Published by Arwen Lynch
Cover design by Chris Savoie of Bayou Cover Designs
Layout by www.formatting4U.com

All rights reserved. No part of this book may be reproduced in any form or by any electronic or mechanical means, including information storage and retrieval systems—except in the case of brief quotations embodied in critical articles or reviews—without permission in writing from the author at readings@tarotbyarwen.com.

For more information on the author and her works, please see www.tarotbyarwen.com

Dedicated to Cai for her friendship and support and to CP for his love and support. And to all the writers published and pre-published, write with joy, y'all.

FOREWORD

You've taken the first step. Now, like the hero and heroines and, yes, even the villains of your stories, you are ready to leave your own Ordinary World behind. This was originally a thirty-three day eCourse. Now you have the ability to work through this at your own pace. You will have lessons, handouts and motivational quotes to guide you and encourage you.

The first and last thing to remember is that you are the creator/creatrix of your world. What you write is good. This book gives you the framework to let your imagination go to work. Build what you hear in your head. Let those characters come to life in the pages of your book.

While the only thing you need for this book is a Tarot deck, I do have a short bibliography for you. I will also suggest a few Tarot decks that I like to use when I'm plotting my own hero's journey for my own works.

Books

- Vogler, Christopher, The Writer's Journey: Mythic Structure for Writers, 3rd edition
- Campbell, Joseph, The Hero with a Thousand Faces (The Collected Works of Joseph Campbell)
- Pearson, Carol, Awakening the Heroes Within: Twelve Archetypes to Help Us Find Ourselves and Transform the World, 1991 *Kindle version*
- Greer, Mary K., Tarot for Yourself *Kindle version*

Tarot Decks

- Radiant Rider-Waite® Tarot, Pamela Colman Smith, U.S. Games Systems Inc
- Joie de Vivre Tarot, Paulina Cassidey, U.S. Games Systems Inc
- Fantastical Creatures Tarot, Lisa Hunt, U.S. Games Systems Inc
- Steampunk Tarot, Barbara Moore, Llewellyn

There are thousands of Tarot decks available. My recommendation is to get a version of the Rider Waite (I add Smith in honor of the artist who was left out for far too long) and one other deck. Get one that appeals to you.

Remember, this isn't about interpretation. It's about imagination. Each card is a springboard for your creative self. Let's jump like the Fool and see what's next.

Contents

Introduction   1
The Cast
    It's Character Building   7
Act I
    The Ordinary World   14
    The Call To Adventure   25
    The Refusal   33
    The Mentor   39
    Crossing The Threshold   46
Act II
    Tests, Enemies and Allies   54
    Approach The Inmost Cave   63
    The Ordeal   71
    The Reward   79
Act III
    The Road Back   87
    Resurrection   95
    Return With The Elixir   103
Encore
    Themes   110
    Journals   118
Tarot Tools
    Major Arcana   122
    Minor Arcana   145
    Court Cards   160
    The Suits   168
    Writers Spreads   186
    The End   193

Introduction: Mapping The Hero's Journey

How a Fool Does Wander

I travel not to go anywhere, but to go. I travel for travel's sake. The great affair is to move.
-- Robert Louis Stevenson

You now hold a map that will show you where your own hero or heroine may wander. You are the cartographer of the tale. You will be in charge of mapping the hero's journey. It will be you who jots in the margins "here there be dragon".

This book is designed to give you thirteen primary lessons plus a few extras to help you discover how to use the system of Tarot as a way to plot your fiction. You can write a short story, a novella or a novel. The length isn't as important as the journey. As Mr. Stevenson says above, the great affair is to move. No one wants to read a stagnant story. The first twelve lessons focus on the Hero's Journey while the thirteenth explores the issue of Theme for a work of fiction.

I'd like to start with a brief history of the Tarot as well as an overview of the Hero's Journey (HJ). I am using the HJ as detailed by Christopher Vogler in The Writer's Journey: Mythic Structure for Writers.

Christopher Vogler took Joseph's Campbell exploration of the monomyth--a cyclical journey or quest undertaken by a mythical hero--and distilled it into twelve steps. We are going to examine each of those steps for our characters by pulling Tarot cards then interpreting them. This will give us a basic outline for our books. More cards can be pulled to move from scene to scene if warranted.

First let's look at the history of Tarot. This is not a history class and Tarot historians have some widely differing opinions on origin and longevity. There are many places on-line and in books for those who want to go deeper into the historical aspect.

Tarot is one of the older forms of divination. Many people believe it to have started with the Egyptians. The first known deck was definitely popularized by the Italians. It was quite popular in 7th century Venice to have a deck created for a specific occasion such as the joining together of two families. The faces in the cards are said to be of the family members of the Visconti and the Sforza ruling clans.

In the late 1800's, the Golden Dawn, a secretive occult society, developed the Celtic Cross spread--or so the story goes. Before this, the most common type of spread would have been a three-card spread or a "Romany" spread.

The Romany spread is usually three rows with five to seven cards per row. The row nearest you is the past. The middle row is the present. The top row would be the future. If you are doing a historical, that would be a more accurate spread. I also do not think that the term "spread" became popular until more recently. More commonly, I believe it was called "throwing the cards" or "laying the cards." You would want to research that though as this is just off-hand information. This spread shares a heritage with the Lenormand tableau layout which uses all 36 cards of the Petit Lenormand.

It is important to understand how you will be using Tarot for this book. Tarot is an intuitive tool. It allows your natural intuition to channel through the cards via the pictures. Think of it as a way to free your right brain. Also note that Tarot is NOT set in stone. Do not let someone read for you if they are not willing to discuss how you can make necessary changes! As I always say, why look at the future if you aren't going to try to change it? Seems like a waste of time to me.

But for this book, you will be using Tarot cards as tools for writing. There is no set meaning when you are doing this. I will offer traditional meanings for cards in this book, but I want to emphasize again that you are using them as tools so your interpretations count most. I encourage you to let your mind wander. This is designed to give you tools to work with rather than creating something for you to lean on.

You will be doing the work in this book at your own pace. You will want to have a notebook (or computer file) that is dedicated to the notes and homework you will do as you progress through these lessons. I include a prompt for writing along with a quote at the end of each chapter. You don't have to do them, but it will help you write a better story if you do. I will refer to this as the journal throughout this book. The technically-minded among you might enjoy using this book with the writing program Scrivener by Latte and Literature.

Joseph Campbell's ground-breaking work, *The Hero with a Thousand Faces*, first laid out the journey of the hero. That book has been used by many writers struggling with how to tell the story that is burning inside of them. Then Vogler stepped in with his book that worked to make it simple for the writer. Here is Vogler's breakdown. Each chapter will expand upon these twelve steps.

ACT I DEPARTURE, SEPARATION
    1. Ordinary World
    2. Call to Adventure
    3. Refusal of the Call
    4. Meeting with the Mentor
    5. Crossing First Threshold

ACT II DESCENT, INITIATION, PENETRATION
    6. Tests, Allies & Enemies
    7. Approach to Inmost Cave
    8. The Ordeal
    9. Reward (Seizing the Sword)

ACT III RETURN
    10. Road Back
    11. Resurrection
    12. Return with Elixir

You can learn more about Vogler's vision in his book, The Writer's Journey. It's on the bibliography in the foreword as well as at the end.

Before we start, you will need a character if you don't have one in mind. An interesting thing about the hero's journey is that you need a hero. And remember, not all heroes begin as heroes. Take Shrek for instance. Now there was an anti-hero for you. That large green misanthrope was the quintessential hermit. When compared to the young, eager Luke Skywalker, you have two very disparate characters. But, and this is a very important "but", they both have the same journey from their ordinary lives to the end where they return with that elixir.

Next I will give you some simple ways to use Tarot to build your character. If you already have a character, you can utilize the first lesson to create layers and depth for your character. The most amazing Hero's Journey will stumble and fall at the gate if your character isn't one your readers want to know more about.

Remember that this is simply a framework for you to develop your story from. There is no hard and fast rule that says you must stick to these steps in this order. It's a poor story that makes too much of its bones and not enough of the story itself. Consider these stages that your Hero should experience but remember that you are the author of your story. You get to say when and how they occur. This framework, this Hero's Journey, has infinite variations. It is the reason that we can have so many different and new stories to read as well as write.

This workbook is designed so that you can use it to start a fresh story or work with a manuscript already in progress. If you have a work in progress (WIP), then you may want to still do each stage to see if you need to anchor the Hero's Journey more in certain places of your manuscript.

I will be using the following films as examples of how the Hero's journey is shown. I highly recommend watching any or all of these movies to break them down. It is important to see what moments seem pivotal to you. Writing is a subjective matter so how you see these movies and the individual Hero's journey may differ from my take.

> Wizard of Oz
> Star Wars
> Shrek
> Avatar

I will draw a card for each step as well as giving examples for each stage's spread. Remember that the focus of this book is to plot your story so focus on the big picture. You can fill in the steps later.

Chapter One
The Cast

It's Character Building

Now let's see about creating a character you can work with. Even if you already have a concept of your main character, I encourage you to use this first lesson to deepen that character. It's a fine balance between creating a character who leaps off the pages and a character who is so perfect your reader can't connect with them.

Create A Character

You cannot dream yourself into a character; you must hammer and forge yourself one.
-- Henry David Thoreau

You must hammer and forge one yourself is quite true of the characters for your stories. You don't want a carbon copy of someone else's character (unless you are writing fan-fic). The Hero of your tale must stand out in your reader's mind. This must be one of the unforgettable things of your book.

It's a toss-up for some as to whether the best tales

are plot-driven or character-driven. I need characters I like. I've heard it said, and it is true for me, that the Hero or Heroine of your book must be someone your reader would want to have lunch with. He or she should be someone who strikes a chord with the reader. Take a minute to write down three characters that come to mind immediately. Now write down three things about each of them that make you remember them.

EXAMPLE:

Scarlet O'Hara is an impetuous, petulant, selfish girl who learns how to be caring too late.

Now I've read some books where the Hero was not someone I could feel sympathy for. But I kept reading because the author managed to hook me into the character somehow. One that stands out in my mind is Stacia Kane's heroine, Chess, from her Downside Ghosts series. Chess is an addict--not really the kind of character you would want to have lunch with, but she is memorable nonetheless. From the movie "Avatar" Jake Scully is not a very good hero at first. One of his flaws is his loyalty to the military.

So how do you create a character that stands out? What do you put into this individual who must be so memorable? It goes beyond hair and eye and skin tone--although an argument for hair could be made by the lead character in "Rapunzel." In the Tarot deck, there are sixteen cards that may help you develop a character. They are the court cards. Each of the four suits has four court cards.

The Court Cards

The Pages represent our youth. They are up to the age of sixteen which has historically been the age of maturity in terms of sexuality. If you get a Page, you might consider that it is in an area where your character is lacking maturity. Traditionally, the Page was the message-carrier so they are often seen by the message they carry. The Page of Swords brings a message of a problem resolution (good or bad.) The Page of Wands delivers news either about a business endeavor or a spiritual matter. The Page of Cups is our lover who brings love letters or Dear John missives. Last is the Page of Coins who could bring a message about health or a job offer.

Next, we have our bold Knights. These are the seventeen—twenty-seven crowd. This is a very mobile group who are seen as travelers. It's one reason you usually see Knights on horses or some type of beast or on some other form of conveyance. A Knight in your Character Spread could indicate a love of travel or perhaps a need to travel. The Knight of Swords represents travel by air. The Knight of Wands goes by motor vehicle including bus, train and motorcycles. The Knight of Cups travels by boat naturally. And the Knight of Coins takes the shank's pony (his own two feet) or an animal.

Queens span the ages of twenty-eight—fifty-five. They are the nurturers as well as the creative force of the court cards. They represent the age where we develop and deepen ourselves. We're usually done with traveling by this time. The Queen of Swords represents one who works in the communication field. The Queen of Wands could be a travel agent or a public relations guru. The Queen of Cups would be the counselor or perhaps the psychic. The Queen of Coins is the high-level manager or tax accountant.

Last are the Kings whose age is fifty-six and beyond. They are the ones who close the deal and make things happen. The King of Swords is the entrepreneur who goes skydiving to brainstorm. Our King of Wands might be a politician with big ideas. The King of Cups is the one who has become a motivational speaker or maybe a guru somewhere. The King of Coins now owns the bank or is a mover-and-shaker in the financial district.

We will be using these for our next exercise. Please remove the court cards from your deck. For this exercise, we will use only the court cards. Shuffle the twelve court cards then draw five for the following exercise.

COURT CHARACTER SPREAD

1. What was your Hero like as a young person?
2. What does your Hero do for a living?
3. Who is your Hero's role model?
4. What is your Hero's weakness?
5. What is your Hero's strength?

EXAMPLE:

1. What was your Hero like as a young person?
The card that I pulled was the Page of Wands. This card traditionally brings the message of being eager and passionate. I would say that my hero was easy to anger and quick to fight.

2. What does your hero do for a living?

I got the Queen of Cups for my male hero. So perhaps he's a male matchmaker or maybe he's a marriage counselor. This is where you will need to be flexible. It could also be his boss or that he works for his mother. I decided he was someone others turned to for comfort in times of emotional distress.

3. Who is your Hero's role model?

Now this card could be called the mentor, but role model is a bit different. This is who he wanted to be when he grew up. The King of Pentacles is the card that I drew. For me, this would be his grandfather who was a bit of a loner after his wife died but never failed to do what his family needed. He made sure they were financially safe.

4. What is your Hero's weakness?

Now we go back to the passion suit of Wands with the Knight of Wands. This card is about victory. He likes to win and sometimes isn't careful about who he insults. This has created some enemies for him.

5. What is your Hero's strength?

Here the King of Cups lends credence to the second card. A counselor or matchmaker who is good at seeing who will make a good match in love would be a good thing. He knows how to keep a secret so maybe he is an investigator?

To bring that all into one package, you have a man who makes his living finding out who's cheating on whom (expressing that Page of Wands passion with the

Queen of Cups) but doesn't have a relationship of his own (King of Pentacles). He wants one like Grandpa and Grandma had, but his current job leaves him with a bad taste in his mouth. He can't talk to anyone about what he does because of confidentiality issues.

At the end of this book you will find some spreads designed to get to know your characters better in a variety of ways. When my writing partner and I are working on a novel, we do spreads on our hero, our heroine and our villain--if there is one. And always remember this one rule.

You are the writer. You are the creator, the creatrix. What develops in your story is from your fertile imagination. Tarot will simply be one more tool in your writer's toolkit. Like any tool, you use it when you need it and lay it aside when you don't. Now let's move into the actual stages of the hero's journey. Grab your cards, your pen, your notebook and jump in.

Throughout this book you will find Journal Prompts. These can be used as you like. I mean for them to provide encouragement to your as a writer. You can think of them as fueling stations. I'll just be adding a little juice to the process as we go along. A helpful tool for this is a timer. Set a timer for ten minutes then just write. Don't think about what you are saying. The energy here is to jump-start your creative process.

#

QUOTE

Who wants to become a writer? And why? Because it's the answer to everything. ... It's the streaming reason

for living. To note, to pin down, to build up, to create, to be astonished at nothing, to cherish the oddities, to let nothing go down the drain, to make something, to make a great flower out of life, even if it's a cactus.
-- Henry David Thoreau

JOURNAL PROMPT

Why do you write? What makes you want to tell a story?

Write with joy, y'all. Remember this book is to help you on your journey to finish your own book. You can do this!

Chapter Two
Act I

The Ordinary World

Everything you want in the world is just outside your comfort zone. Everything you could possibly want.
-- Jennifer Aniston

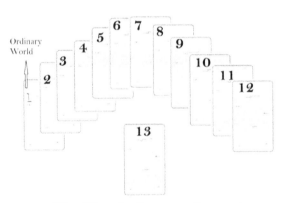

The Hero's Journey Layout

It has been said that all stories must have a hero's journey. I would disagree. All stories do not need a hero's journey. All good stories do, though. Even the tale of those three little pigs has a hero's journey as Corey Green, M.Ed. points out in a presentation given at the 2009 IRA Annual Convention *Copyright 2009 Corey Green. Presented at 2009 IRA Annual Convention in Phoenix, February 21-25 Visit CoreyGreen.com for more writing resources.

The Hero's Journey is a monomyth. This is a description of a basic pattern found in many narratives from around the world. To learn more about how and why Joseph Campbell came up with this, you should read his book The Hero with a Thousand Faces (Bollingen Series.) The first edition was published in 1949 and it continues to be a popular book for authors. With good reason as it delineates this journey in an unforgettable way.

What Campbell did was give parameters to something all good story tellers knew. Campbell named the building blocks of a story. Another book I highly recommend is The Writers Journey: Mythic Structure for Writers, 3rd Edition. Vogler filters Campbell's work through a more detailed lens focusing on the fictional story. I use the Tarot as a way to apply color, depth and layers to those building blocks.

For the purposes of this discussion, I will use Hero as predominantly genderless even though I will default to "he" as the pronoun. The journey can be the hero's journey or the heroine's journey or even the villain's journey. Protagonist and antagonist both have journeys through every good story. Sometimes these journeys parallel one another in odd ways. Never forget that the hero and heroine (if you have both) have unique journeys as well. What is good for your heroine goose may not be good for your hero gander.

The first step is the Ordinary World which is the ordinary mundane existence of the Hero. He knows his place in the world--whether he likes it or not. The very commonness of his world will stand in strict contrast to where he must journey. But what is common to the pauper is unusual to the prince. Don't limit yourself by pigeonholing "ordinary".

Think of this in terms of yourself. Your background is part of who you are. This is part of your Ordinary World. Getting up and going to work may be part of your Ordinary World. This is a very important position because here we think about the back story. Who is this Hero and how did he get to where he is? Is he content in his Ordinary World and yanked out of it or does he express dissatisfaction about his surroundings longing to be anywhere but there? You use this to give hints of the Hero's backstory without dumping it all in one spot.

I have pulled information from my own knowledge as well as other sources. My Ordinary World consists of my home, my job, my pets, going to the grocery store, doing laundry. All these things make my everyday world. If you were to place me in a penthouse apartment with servants and an unending bank balance, you would be thrusting me into a special world just as surely as if you took away my home and money. This is important because the Ordinary World by default must be looked back on from time to time to remind the Hero of where he's come from and how far he's gotten. Sometimes this is a reality check.

Often the Hero chafes at his existence in this Ordinary World. He knows something else is out there--like Dorothy in the Wizard of Oz or Luke in Star Wars. They both knew they had to seek some intangible, indefinable thing. Neither was satisfied with the status quo. Only one, Luke, had a clear picture of what that dissatisfaction was. For him, it was the fact that the Rebel Alliance was "out there" and he was not. Dorothy's unhappiness stemmed from her dog being threatened by the mean Miss Gulch. Her Ordinary World changed when Toto's life was in danger.

This position can be seen as the Emperor, the fourth card in the Major Arcana. Four is the number of hard work in numerology. The Emperor is the father figure in the Tarot. He is the sign of Aries which is the head in the astrological body. Consider that the Ordinary World is the parent energy while your Hero is the child wanting to be free of the rules.

Astrologically speaking, Aries is the starter. This is the sign of the initiator who works within the rules and structures of society as the Hero knows it. You could think of it as the Emperor being an actual figure in the story. This Emperor is not kind or moderate in his judgments and must be taken down so that a better world can emerge. He is a fence that corrals your hero's action. He impedes forward movement.

The Wizard of Oz's Dorothy demonstrates this energy very well. Likewise, Jake Sully (Avatar) chafes against the restrictions of being confined to a wheelchair. Shrek's Ordinary World shows him to be content in his swamp if a bit annoyed by all the shrieking when he's just out for a walk. All these Heroes rebel in some way against the current authority in their Ordinary World.

The Hero represents the flaw in the Ordinary World. There will be a flaw. Why else would your Hero leave his safe, comfortable world? He is often not aware of what is wrong. Something just doesn't feel right. Again, this could be a person in your story or it could be some other intangible thing. Maybe your hero is just a simple rabbit who only wants a meal. His Ordinary World is clover but he longs for the farmer's carrots as does Peter Rabbit from Beatrice Potter's whimsical stories.

Now think about your character and your setting. If you know things about your initial setting already, write it down. If not, don't worry. This can be a way to spark some thoughts. Think about their birthday. Here is a brief list of some astrological key phrases.

> Aries -- I am
> Taurus -- I have
> Gemini -- I think
> Cancer -- I feel
> Leo -- I will
> Virgo -- I analyze
> Libra -- I balance
> Scorpio -- I desire
> Sagittarius -- I understand
> Capricorn -- I use
> Aquarius -- I know
> Pisces -- I believe

For the rest of this journey you will be using your full deck, **minus each card you draw for the stages of your book**. There are also spreads for each step of the journey. You will want to use the full deck for these spreads as well. Because of this, it may be easier to have a deck that you use for the spreads so that you don't have to keep re-locating your Hero's Journey cards each time. That will be a matter of personal preference of course.

In the Tarot world there are many ways to shuffle. Some will even tell you never to shuffle at all. Again, personal preference will lead you. Here is how I shuffle. I offer this as one way of doing it. I do recommend that you shuffle the same way each time. It creates a muscle memory that can also trigger your brain to think "Hey! It's writing time."

Split your deck in half. Riffle the left side and the right side together. This is also called poker shuffling. It is the way most of us shuffle playing cards. Focus on your question--in this case, your character. Shuffle as long as you feel necessary. My preference is no fewer than three but no more than seven.

When you feel ready, and before the cards are worn completely paper-thin, cut your deck into three piles. I advocate for using the hand you do not write with. For me that would be my left hand since I am right handed. Place the piles left to right (if you are left-handed, it would be right to left.) The point of this is to shift your brain from the mundane world to the creative world.

Next restack your cards by starting with the last pile you created. That stack will be the top stack. If this is all too confusing, make it simple.

1. Shuffle
2. Cut the cards into three piles
3. Restack the cards so that last pile you made is on top of the newly stacked deck.

Now, turn the top card up.

This is your hero's Ordinary World. This is the mundane, every day that he lives in. In this card is a clue to what is causing him to chafe at the bit. What is making him want to wander, to move, to explore.

DO NOT LOOK UP THE MEANING! I mean this. Remember that this is not about memorizing the cards and using traditional meanings. You are using Tarot to free your mind. You are allowing your Muse a different way to speak. For my purposes, the Muse is that creative part of ourselves. He or she may need music as you write or maybe silence. You will hear many writers complain that their Muse has taken a vacation. Using Tarot as writing tool can cut that vacation short.

> Back to the card you just drew.
> Examine the card.

- What do you see in the background?
- What is in the foreground?
- What symbols are in the card?
- What do these symbols mean to you?

Your journal will serve you well here. Write down your first impressions. Mark this entry Ordinary World in your journal. You might even like to sketch the card in your journal.

Don't worry if things don't make sense. This is a beginning not an end. Once you have gathered up what you see in this card and written it down, then and only then can you open the LWB (Little White Book) or companion book. Read what is in there. See what you can add to what you already got for this card. Understand that just like your own book, the deck you use has an author and often a separate artist. Together they have a vision for their deck and meanings. You are using their work as a leaping off place. Don't box yourself in with their meanings. Remember that you are the author of your story.

If you want basic meanings for each care, you can also refer to the two chapters on the meanings of the Major Arcana and the Minor Arcana. These are in the Tarot Tools section of this book.

Take a moment to explore what you wrote. Here is a formula you can use to draw out more from each card. I use this template throughout this book. It can be used as a starting point for your synopsis once you are done with the book. Additionally, I like doing a spread for each step of the Hero's Journey. I find that I can dig in deeper. You will find the spread first and then the story template. Use what you find in the spread to fill out your story template.

ORDINARY WORLD SPREAD

- Hold the card that you drew for your Ordinary World out.
- Shuffle the deck at least 3-5 times.
- Cut the deck into three piles.
- Restack them so that the last cut is on top.
- Draw two cards.
- Lay the first one facedown to the left of the Ordinary World.
- Lay the second one facedown to the right of the Ordinary World.

Card One
Ordinary World Card
Card Two

Card One (to the left) is what your Hero loves about the Ordinary World. This is what is comfortable and known. This is Dorothy's bedroom and familiar surroundings. What do you see in this card that would make your Hero happy? This is why he would want to stay.

Card Two (to the right) is what your Hero feels is lacking about the Ordinary World. This is what chafes. This is Dorothy's singing "Somewhere Over The Rainbow" as she dreams of something--anything--different. Here is where you look for what he might want. If you don't see things your hero wants, look for things that your hero would dislike enough to want to leave.

STORY TEMPLATE:

My hero, (name), starts out in a world represented by (card). This card looks like (description here) to me. It makes me feel (emotion here). My hero's everyday life is (description here) according to this card. The biggest problem I see with this card is (description here) because my hero needs to (action.)

Let yourself expand on these ideas. Do not be trapped by the formula. It is only a start for you. You may branch out. In fact, it's encouraged since you want to know as much as you can about this starting point. It's best not to start the next chapter until you've done this step. Really dive into this part.

TIP: Backstory dump is a term used in fiction writing. It is when a writer feels a need to tell you the character's entire history. In general, it will cause an editor or agent to get bored fast. That's a very bad thing in the publishing world.

Think of a time when you met someone in a social

setting. You introduced yourself. They then take up a good half hour or more of your time telling you about themselves from birth to now. They don't leave out any details.

Besides being glassy-eyed with boredom, you also have no need to ask them questions. They have left you no opportunity to enjoy the "getting to know you" part of a relationship. Don't do that to your reader. What you learn about your hero's Ordinary World doesn't need to be handed over to the reader. Dribble in bits of that as you build your story.

Also, here is a good place to jot down a physical description of your character. You can file this in a document that you might refer to as your "Story Bible". It's a good thing to have.

EXAMPLE:

My writing partner, Cai Smith, and I did a Hero's Journey spread for the hero of our third book, Changing Focus (Marilu Mann). Micah Keeps Vigil is a wolf shifter who works as a bounty hunter.

His Ordinary World card was the Six of Swords. This card has a theme of taking care of others and coming home. Micah's story opens with him returning home after being away. He has come home to rest and to take care of some business.

QUOTE

When I sit down to write a book, I do not say to myself, 'I am going to produce a work of art.' I write it because there is some lie that I want to expose, some

fact to which I want to draw attention, and my initial concern is to get a hearing.
    -- George Orwell

JOURNAL PROMPT

What do you need to draw attention to with your story? What needs to be heard?

Write with joy, y'all. Every day put words on the page. Don't let your inFERNAL editor stop you. Now is the time to write forward. You can edit later. Promise!

Chapter Three

The Call to Adventure

Take the adventure, heed the call, now ere the irrevocable moment passes! 'Tis but a banging of the door behind you, a blithesome step forward, and you are out of your old life and into the new!
-- Kenneth Grahame

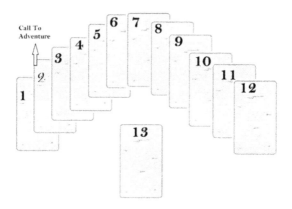

The next step in our Hero's Journey is that clarion call to adventure. Here the Hero is jolted out of his comfortable world. There is something that must be done and only he can do it. It might be the Hero out jogging and tripping over a dead body or finding out his father was a Jedi Knight or learning that her dog is going to be killed. Maybe his brother was killed and he is needed on another planet. What if some ruler confines a bunch of fairy tale creatures to his swamp? Someone has to do something. And that someone must be your Hero even if he really would rather not be bothered.

Whatever this moment is, it must be life-changing. It is utterly disruptive to the Hero's Ordinary World. But, as Kenneth Grahame puts it, you need to heed the call before the moment passes. This is the moment in the book where your reader begins to identify with your character. Remember the Ordinary World and what is chafing. This call will alleviate that itch eventually. At first, it may appear to only make things worse.

In the Tarot, this step has been associated with the Hierophant, the number five card, but I don't agree with that. This is a challenge not a rule. For me the Hierophant represents rules and structure. While I can see this as the Hero needing to go against the existing rules, I am not sure that the Hierophant is an active enough card for this step. Interestingly enough the numerological meanings for the number five might make you think of a salesman. A five personality is said to be great for parties because of their originality and great conversational skills. Not what I associate with the Hierophant which was the Pope in the older decks and still is in many decks today.

I would have to say that the Call to Adventure is

the Fool because this is about impulsive behaviors and taking chances. You must take a chance when you answer the Call to Adventure because you could potentially lose everything you hold dear. The killer might kill you. You might not make it as a Jedi. Your dog might die even if you do run away.

This is a classic pushmi-pullyu moment. You want to go. You can't go. You know you need to go because of the bad things that will happen if you stay. You know you can't go because of the bad things that might happen if you don't stay.

The Fool is the 0 card. It is the only card in a traditional Tarot deck with no number associated. Numerology is an important aspect of Tarot. For me, zero represents all the possibilities in the world. It is the completion and the beginning of all things. The circle is unending. I could go on and on about how circles affect me. I could even sing you one of my favorite folk songs about how "all my life's a circle." I'll spare you that though.

An important thing about the Fool is that it neither starts nor finishes the Major Arcana. Rather, it does both. As the Zero card, he is the connector card in the Tarot. But it is the Fool's reputation as the one who takes risks that makes it the perfect card for this Call to Adventure.

This is a step that should create urgency for your hero. What is strong enough to pull your Hero off his proverbial couch and--at the very least--get him to answer the doorbell? What motivates him to step outside of himself? Think of this as the cutting of the umbilical cord that ties our Hero to the Ordinary World. He must be willing to take a chance.

This card will sometimes show the actual problem or challenge. It can also be seen as how he will answer the call. Will your Hero be the "grab the white horse and armor and go" heroine or the "let's sit down and think about this" hero?

What is the problem your Hero must answer? Is an evil cloud gathering on the horizon? Does an army threaten his home? Has a disease broken out on her spaceship? For Luke, it was joining with Obi Wan Kenobi to answer Leia's request for help. In Wizard of Oz it is Dorothy running away to save Toto's life. For the classic anti-hero, Shrek, his Call to Adventure is actually when the other fairy tale creatures are dumped into his swamp. He's not happy about it, but he's going to have to go somewhere to fix the problem. Jake Sully, Marine, needs money for new legs, but that means filling in for his dead scientist twin.

Joseph Campbell states, "A blunder--apparently the merest chance--reveals an unsuspected world, and the individual is drawn into a relationship with forces that are not rightly understood".

Your Hero doesn't necessarily want to do this but he knows something must be done. The Hero has to decide to be the one to step up to the plate and make things happen. Without him getting involved, he realizes that the Ordinary World he knows may be irreparably changed.

Now let's pull a card for the Call to Adventure. First, remove the card you pulled for your Hero's Ordinary World if you put it back in the deck. Maybe you could put each card in your journal as a book mark. Another thought is to get a large corkboard. I don't like pin holes in my cards so I would crisscross it with ribbon to tuck the cards in as I draw them. You can have a visual representation of your story arc to work from this way.

Whatever you do with that first card, don't put it back in the deck because you don't want to get the same card twice. Talk about back story!

Focus on what you know about your character. See him as real in your mind. Consider where he is in his Ordinary World. Shuffle the deck as before including cutting the deck into three piles. Turn over the top card once you have restacked the deck.

What do you see? Think about this as a pictorial letter. Someone has slipped this card under your Hero's door. What do they see? What does the card tell them? Write about this for a bit. Let your mind wander down rabbit holes. Include what ifs. As a writer, you should consider the "what if" game a constant companion. What if Shrek meets a talking donkey? What if Dorothy finds a tin man? What if Luke is befriended by a smuggler?

Now pull out the book that came with the deck. Read the description. Does it add to your take on the card? Write it down. Fill out the holes you might have had. Or don't use any of it. If it doesn't make sense, it doesn't make sense, right? No need to pound a square card into a round position!

Now let's write a bit. You might use this formula as a leaping off point.

SPREAD: CALL TO ADVENTURE

1. Start with the card you just pulled for your Call to Adventure. You can put your Ordinary World card back in or leave it out.

2. Shuffle the deck at least 3-5 times.
3. Cut the deck into three piles.
4. Restack them so that the last cut is on top. (Steps 2-4 will be referred to as Shuffle and Cut for the next lessons)
5. Draw two cards.
6. Lay the first one facedown to the left of the Call to Adventure card.
7. Lay the second one facedown to the right of the Call to Adventure card.

Card One
Call to Adventure Card
Card Two

Card One (to the left) represents what precipitates the Call to Adventure. What is happening when the Call comes? You can see this as an actual activity or as the goal of the hero before he got the Call. Shrek's goal before his Call to Adventure was simply to be left alone.

Card Two (to the right) represents why your character would consider accepting this call. What piques his interest to the point that he wants to know more? Using Shrek here again, he answers the call in order to achieve his goal of being left alone. If you've seen the movie, you know that goal changes drastically once he meets Fiona.

The cards that you pull for these optional clarifying spreads will be put back into the deck (minus the Journey Cards) before you shuffle for the next step of your Hero's Journey.

STORY TEMPLATE:

My hero, (name), started out in a world represented by (card). Now s/he has been called to adventure by (the card). When I look at this card, I see (items in the card). These make me think about (actions/people/things) that my hero might take or meet. The fear of leaving the Ordinary World is represented by (something on this card or about this card). The need to leave the Ordinary World is represented by (something on this card or about this card).

As before, expand. Write past the margins. Scribble over the boundaries. Revisits to the Ordinary World should be brief if you must but this is about moving forward so don't spend too much time there. Complete this part before moving on to the next lesson.

EXAMPLE:

For Micah, we drew the Six of Cups. This card shows two people who are courting one another. They are often shown standing on stone to reference a strong foundation. Micah meets Olivia. He is very attracted to her but she doesn't accept his interest. His Ordinary World is shaken because here is a woman who doesn't seem to pick up on his signals.

TIP: Here is a good place to let some more back story out by letting your character reminisce about things. Micah tells Olivia a little about his background but the reader learns more about him from what he decides to not tell her.

If you like, you can do the following spread to learn more about your Hero's Call to Adventure.

QUOTE

There is no greater agony than bearing an untold story inside you.
 -- Maya Angelou

JOURNAL PROMPT

What untold stories are inside you? Write down five ideas then tuck them away for a rainy, blocked day.

Write with joy, y'all. The best sentence a writer ever hears is not "I want to publish your book." It's "What else do you have?" Always write. Even when your book is lingering with an agent or editor, you should be working on your next amazing story. What else do you have? That's what you want to hear.

Chapter Four

The Refusal

Remember what Bilbo used to say: It's a dangerous business, Frodo, going out your door. You step onto the road, and if you don't keep your feet, there's no knowing where you might be swept off to.
-- JRR Tolkien

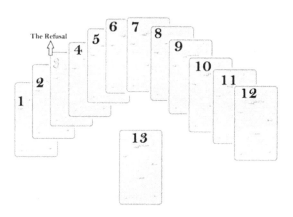

Lesson three begins with what I like to call the Donkey Moment. This is where the Hero may have made a move forward then suddenly says, "Oh HELL NO. I am not going!" He jerks back trying to get to his Ordinary World again. Sometimes this comes out as a minor reluctance while other times it is a huge ugly tug-of-war between what the Hero knows needs to be done and his own insecurities.

This is the card that shows you what your Hero fears. Not an external "big bad guy with a sword in his hand" fear but an internal "what if I fall down" fear. He knows if he proceeds forward, he will change irrevocably. This change may render him unable to every return to the safety of his Ordinary World.

Take a moment to put yourself in that position. You accept this quest—this *geas*—this challenge and you can NEVER return to the home you know. Beyond a shadow of a doubt, the Ordinary World will never be what it was before this moment. And, if the Hero is honest with himself, the Ordinary World began to change the moment he noticed something wasn't right.

The home will still be there, but you, the Hero, know on a cellular level that it will never be the same. Consider Bilbo Baggins as he leaves the Shire in JRR Tolkien's "The Hobbit". He is off on an adventure yet he knows as he leaves his familiar home--nothing will be the same. Dorothy's refusal is not the moment she runs away. It comes when she tries to go home again. Shrek brilliantly refuses by battling the knights not realizing that he's actually showing he is the right ogre for the job.

In this crucial part of your plot your reader learns about more than the external risks for your Hero. The internal risks are magnified here. This is one of the places your readers must buy into your Hero's journey.

They have to want to turn the page because suddenly they are walking beside Dorothy. It's important to them to see how Shrek will save the princess. They have to see what Bilbo finds.

It is the beginning of the struggle. This is when you can first start torturing and twisting your hero. The Hero doesn't want to but you, and your readers, know he will have to. Rub your hands together while chuckling evilly if you like. You are the mad scientist charting out his path.

The Major Arcana card I associate with this is the Lovers. Now, you might think this an odd card until you know that Gemini rules this card. Think pushmi-pullyu again. There is an internal war doing on for the Hero. He knows on that fundamental level that he has to do this, but he has been cursed with the knowledge of what could happen if everything goes horribly wrong.

The Lovers more often represents a spiritual partnership rather than a physical one. The Gemini twins were Castor and Pollux. When one died, the other was so lost that he asked the Gods to allow him to be with his brother. This is one reason the Lovers is more of a spiritual card. The Two of Cups is the physical card of love, in case you were interested.

Something to note here is that these steps of the Hero's Journey don't always happen in this order. It's fairly common, but don't worry if your Refusal comes after your Mentor. This is your story and you are the cartographer. If you want your road to double back, then double the heck back!

One common thing is that the Hero doesn't listen to the Call to Adventure. He doesn't "buy in" to the idea that he really is needed. This moment of refusal is when he gets what he could lose. The Hero who rushes off the moment the Call comes in will have some moment that makes him totally reevaluate why he ever left his Ordinary World.

Consider the enthusiastic young soldier who enlists at the beginning of a war. What are his reactions to killing his first man? Mortality rears its ugly head and he has to realize that if things had gone another way, he'd be the one lying dead at the feet of the other soldier.

Refusals are also not static, one-time things. Reluctant heroes drag their feet a lot. Indiana Jones is a great reluctant hero because he just wants the artifact. He doesn't want to save the girl, the world, the universe. He just wants to get what he came to get and go back to teaching. In Avatar, Jake Sully only wants to get his legs back so he isn't really invested in anyone else's problems. He doesn't want to be the hero that the N'avi need. And he doesn't fully commit until the Home Tree comes down.

This is a lesson in learning what the real challenge is. Maybe it wasn't what the Hero originally thought. Think about what is preventing the Hero from seeing what the real challenge is. And remember that once he realizes what the call truly is, he cannot avoid taking responsibility for the action.

Not to harp but this is a fear card because the Hero must overcome his fears. In Star Wars Luke refuses by insisting he return to his aunt and uncle's farm. What greeted him there? His home destroyed with his aunt and uncle dead. This motivated him and gave him reason to really hate the Empire on a very personal level. Suddenly this Adventure isn't someone else's. It is very personal and very real.

Think of this as the fear and commitment card. I

know that's a bit of a dichotomy. How about the "suck it up" card? No matter how bad things look, they are worse if you turn back.

As before, shuffle your deck and cut the cards. Draw the top card and let yourself go.

Now it is time to look at this card. I want you to delve into this. Write about it. Let your mind wander. You might use this formula as a leaping off point.

THE REFUSAL SPREAD

1. Hold the card that you drew for your Refusal out.
2. Please note that you will be leaving all of the cards for the main Hero's Journey out and shuffling the rest back in if you choose to do these spreads.
3. Shuffle the deck at least 3-5 times.
4. Cut the deck into three piles.
5. Restack them so that the last cut is on top.
6. Draw two cards.
7. Lay the first one facedown to the left of the Refusal card.
8. Lay the second one facedown to the right of the Refusal card.

Card One
Refusal Card
Card Two

Card One (to the left) represents your Hero's biggest fear about answering that Call to Adventure. It is what motivates him to refuse. What can he lose permanently if he doesn't turn his back? Jake Sully could lose his chance to have his mobility back.

Card Two (to the right) represents what responsibilities can't be abandoned in order to answer the Call to Adventure. It is why he can't refuse. For Jake Sully, it goes beyond the love he has for Neytiri. He understands that it is his fault that Home Tree was destroyed. He has to make it right because he really has become one of the N'avi.

STORY TEMPLATE:

My hero, (name), started out in a world represented by (card). Now he has been called to adventure by (the card). But he refuses because (what reason does the card suggest?) The worst thing that could happen if he goes is (something from the card). The worst thing that could happen if he doesn't go is (something from the card here.)

Let your Muse have her moment. Color outside the lines. Look at the three cards to see if there are any symbols on all three. Maybe one color stands out. With three cards of your Hero's journey drawn, patterns may begin to emerge. Something on this card could make you change your mind about the call. That's okay. Jot that down as a possibility. Complete this part before moving on to the next lesson.

QUOTE

Each writer is born with a repertory company in his head. Shakespeare has perhaps 20 players. ... I have 10 or so, and that's a lot. As you get older, you become more skillful at casting them.
-- Gore Vidal

JOURNAL PROMPT

Who are the voices in your head? How do you hear your characters? What do they sound like?

Write with joy, y'all. These are your characters. It's your voice. Find pictures to represent your characters and post them where you can look at them.

Chapter Five

The Mentor

First learn stand, then learn fly. Nature rule, Daniel-san, not mine
 -- Mr. Miyagi from Karate Kid

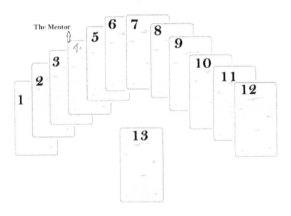

QUICK! Name three mentors from popular fiction such as movies or books. Don't think about this. Just rattle off, or write down, three.

I'll bet you guessed Yoda or Obi Wan Kenobi as

one of the three, right? It's hard not to because Star Wars has become so ingrained in our psyche. Maybe you went for Albus Dumbledore if you are more the Harry Potter type. What about a less easily identified mentor figure? Maybe Gordon Gekko from Wall Street is more your style?

Here we go into one of the most well-known moments of the Hero's Journey. Mentors are something most of us are familiar with as an iconic archetype. A mentor is a teacher but more than a teacher. The good ones tend to be very close to the Hero. They often take a parental role or that of a trusted advisor.

But you should remember that mentors aren't always good people. Sometimes they teach us what not to do by showing us the consequences. Hannibal Lector for instance can be a Mentor. He's a villain but he teaches the heroine in Silence of the Lambs through his examples. What role did Severus Snape play? Consider Vito Corleone from The Godfather as a brilliantly evil mentor figure.

Can a Hero have more than one Mentor? Of course he can. Just look at Luke with Obi Wan and Yoda and even Han Solo to some extent. Each of those served as a mentor on his journey. Obi Wan is the most traditional of those since he died. Death is a very common way to move past the Mentor.

Also, just to make this even more confusing, the Mentor is not always a physical person. Sometimes it is an object or perhaps an animal of mystical abilities. This Mentor comes to the Hero (or the Hero comes to him-- Mohammed? Mountain. Mountain? Mohammed.) to bring him confidence, advice or some type of training. Maybe it is a magical flying carpet or a faithful old dog (Old Yeller, anyone?) Whatever it is, this Mentor is here to help the Hero overcome the fears Card Three (Refusal) brought up.

In the Tarot, I see the Hermit as the Mentor card. Others have mentioned the Chariot, but that is mastery of self. I can see that as a type of Mentor. For me, as a fiction writer, I want my Mentor to be more tangible. The Hermit is the one who studies away from the noise of the Ordinary World. He is apart from the mundane on many levels even if he is visible. Albus Dumbledore from Harry Potter's world is a perfect example of this type of hermit. Even though he is Headmaster, he still has secrets that are only revealed later.

In the first book of the Lusting Wild series, Changing Times, (oh no random plugging of book), Cai and I made one of Tony's friends the Mentor to both Tony and to the heroine Carly. This character is the hero of book three which tells you he doesn't meet with the traditional end of the Mentor. But Micah is removed from Tony's world by several factors. He is not from New Orleans. He is Native American. He has a power other shifters don't possess. He is apart from them but still a part of them.

You may wonder why the teachers usually have to die. It's for character motivation, darlings. And, even more importantly for me, it's for reader buy-in. Show the Hero, poor sad Hero, struggling with big bad nasty fears. Cue the Mentor. Enter a kindly old man or a curmudgeonly wizard or a gun-toting fed or a strange suit-wearing man named K. Let him or her guide the Hero through the Refusal and get them to the other side. Then we kill the Mentor leaving the Hero alone yet again.

ET Voila`! You've created instant sympathy from the reader if you do it right. But we are not going to kill the Mentor yet! Our Hero needs his Mentor. This will propel him into the next part of the story.

Consider that here, on this part of the Journey, the Hero must overthrow his attachment to his Ordinary World, fully answer the Call to Adventure and overcome his own Refusal. Big order for our Hero, no? He needs someone (or something) to help him.

This can manifest as Yoda training Luke in the swamp or Arthur being given Excalibur. Even Jaws has a mentor figure in Robert Shaw's crusty seadog who knows all about sharks. And like I said, not all mentors are sweet. Most offer the hero a much-needed kick in the butt to get him moving in the right direction.

"When the student is ready, the teacher will appear."

This is an adage I learned from a teacher of mine. I have found it to be very true. If I was actively looking for a teacher, I often didn't find them. But the moment I stopped, someone would show up. The Hero will also learn that once he has committed to the quest, consciously or unconsciously, his Mentor will show up.

That moment of commitment is huge. You need to anchor the hero with this. Make it so big that he can't screw it up. Even if he is the bumbling, inept sort of hero I personally find quite endearing. He needs this because it brings him to his Mentor.

Now who or what is your Hero's Mentor? Remember that this can be a non-human character such as Aladdin's flying carpet or Arthur's sword. When you examine the card you pull, don't lock yourself into Obi Wan Kenobi. Remember Old Yeller and Excalibur could show up here as well.

Shuffle the cards. Cut the cards into three piles then restack them. Pull the top card.

Now look at this card. What jumps out at you first? Remember that this lesson is for you to write about the card and what you see. Try to imagine how your Hero feels when presented with this Mentor. Relief? Shock? Horror? Recognition?

Now it's time to head back to your journal or word document to write. You might use this formula as a leaping off point.

THE MENTOR SPREAD

1. Hold the card that you drew for your Mentor out.
2. Please note that you will be leaving all of the cards for the main Hero's Journey out and shuffling the rest back in if you choose to do these spreads.
3. Shuffle the deck at least 3-5 times.
4. Cut the deck into three piles.
5. Restack them so that the last cut is on top.
6. Draw two cards.
7. Lay the first one facedown to the left of the Mentor.
8. Lay the second one facedown to the right of the Mentor.

Card One
Mentor Card
Card Two

Card One (to the left) represents how the Hero sees the Mentor at first. This is that initial impression and gut reaction. This card may physically describe the Mentor but don't dismiss the idea that it shows you the internal Mentor or how the Hero perceives the Mentor. It may not be a good first meeting. Luke already knew his Mentor as Old Ben who his uncle said was "just a crazy old man."

Card Two (to the right) offers what the most important lesson the Hero will learn from the Mentor. For better or worse, the Mentor must impart lessons that will change the Hero. Remember that this piece of your story is how the Hero learns to answer the Call to Adventure. For Luke Skywalker, it is the death of Obi Wan Kenobi that moves him from farm boy to Jedi Knight.

STORY TEMPLATE:

My hero, (name), started out in a world represented by (card). Now he has been called to adventure by (the card). But he refuses because (what reason does the card suggest?) The worst thing that could happen if he goes is (something from the card). Now add in what he will learn from his Mentor (card) or what/who his Mentor is.

Let your Muse have her moment. Don't worry about what you write. This is exploration. Remember the pattern you may have seen in the first three. Check to see if this shows a repetition or if you see something new. Complete this part before moving on to the next lesson.

You are now a third of the way through the twelve steps of the Hero's Journey. Take a moment to review what you've written for each of the four first steps. Examine all four cards for any recurring images or symbols. If you have something that repeats, what does that symbol mean to you? What does it mean to your hero?

EXAMPLE:

Here we drew the Sun. This was an interesting card for a Mentor and a good example of what happens when you get a non-human Mentor. Or, in this case, a lot of Mentors. The Sun represents home and family. Here, Micah's teacher was his pack. He learned how to cross his threshold because he wanted family.

QUOTE

Just write every day of your life. Read intensely. Then see what happens. Most of my friends who are put on that diet have very pleasant careers.
-- Ray Bradbury

JOURNAL PROMPT

What does "read intensely" mean to you? How does that affect your writing?

Write with joy, y'all. Consider this. If 250 words a day is a page, then if you write just 250 words a day, in a year you will have 88000 words. Keep writing.

Chapter Six

Crossing The Threshold

The teacher who is indeed wise does not bid you to enter the house of his wisdom but rather leads you to the threshold of your mind.
-- Khalil Gibran

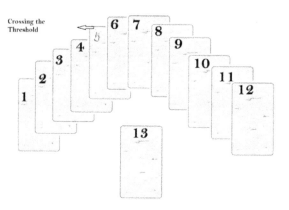

And isn't that quote perfect for this moment in the Hero's Journey. His interaction with the Mentor brings him to the point of crossing the threshold. I want to start with a definition. I tend to see threshold and think of the bottom of the door we step through. I knew that wasn't really what was meant here. I turned to one of the writer's best friends--the dictionary.

The starting point for a new state or experience

Each piece of the journey is important, but this one is very important. Here is where you re-hook your reader if they are not fully invested yet. Consider this a type of Big Black Moment because this is going to change everything. The reason the Hero hesitated was because he still understood what he could lose. Now he understands the bigger picture. It isn't about him losing the farm. It's about an evil overlord blowing up planets.

Our Hero has to have fully, and finally, committed to his part on this Journey. One thing to note here is to compare this to your other Hero (if you have one) and see if they are in accord or discord with one another. This will be a story line in and of itself if they are juxtaposed, yes? I do a spread for my hero and my heroine. The villain gets a spread as well if there is to be a bad guy. The conflict in your story isn't always another person. It can be so many other things. For instance, a hero and heroine fighting to survive during a blizzard casts the weather as the villain.

This is the gateway card. It marks the spot where the Hero will cross from his Ordinary World into the Special World. Think of this as the "no turning back" card. This is the Millennium Falcon's jump into hyperspace. Some say this is where Dorothy put her feet on the yellow brick road. For me, it is when she committed to helping the scarecrow. At that point, in my opinion, she had an obligation to move forward.

The Tarot card some associate here is the Strength card. I can agree with this because one of the meanings here is mastering the beast which can be seen as mastering fear. However, I would also offer that the Chariot is a good card here since it is about mastering of self and marshaling your forces. You have to pick up the reins and drive now. Which do you prefer here?

Crossing The Threshold is not easy. If you are a Tarot reader, think of this as the Block card in the Celtic Cross. If you are a writer, think of this as one of the places your Hero's motivation/conflict may change. He's responded to the Call to Adventure. He's had the moment of Refusal. His Mentor has patted him on his head or kicked him in the rump (or both) and prepared him.

Now it's up to the Hero. This is why I would use the Chariot here rather than Strength. It's more important that my Hero is now acknowledging that he is engaged in the struggle. Another issue is that the Chariot is often pulled by animals looking in opposite dircctions. This reminds me as a writer that my hero may still feel pulled one way or the other.

One keyword for the Chariot is "Mastery". Since Strength is about mastering the beast self, this mastery is more about the intellectual self. For your Hero to fully cross this threshold, he must have mastered his own thoughts. Here is a good point in the story to demonstrate a flaw your hero may have.

Do note that when I say somewhere is a good point that I don't mean just do it once and leave it. You may not "hit it and quit it." It's important to think of your story in layers. Many things should be multi-layered so that when your heroine bakes a cake, she can be plotting to burn it so the hero won't fall in love with her. Always remember that every scene should add to the story somehow. It needs to propel the action forward.

Remember that not only must you address the hero's conflict both from an external aspect--who is that woman and why does she have a three-layered chocolate cake leveled at my temple? You also must address the internal conflict--I can't let her see how scared I am. Keep in mind the motivation on both levels as well. In this scene, external would be "get away so I can stay safe" while internal might be "I have to live so I can get Timmy out of that well."

Also, (cue spooky *dun dun dunnnn* music here) this is the moment of the Shadow. No, not "The Shadow Knows" hero, but the Shadow villain (or internal shadow self which can be a worse villain) is triggered/released when the Hero Crosses The Threshold. Think of it as our Hero tripping an alarm system. The enemy now knows the Hero is not going back. He has thrown down a glove to challenge the Shadow. Realize that the Hero may not even know he's triggered this alarm. He could be cluelessly tripping over a bed of snakes. He won't know a thing until the first one strikes.

Even when the Shadow is a real character, the Hero has to acknowledge some piece of his own shadow and vanquish it before he can go on to defeat the visible Shadow. In the book of the first (or last depending on your point of view) three Star Wars movies, Luke had to grapple with the idea that his father was the evil mastermind behind the Empire's takeover of the known universe. Or at least his father was the weapon wielded by the Emperor. He had to recognize that he, too, could be as bad as his father.

When the Shadow is alerted to the Hero's Crossing the Threshold, it is not unusual to have some pushback. This is an action point because the Hero often must do battle with either the Shadow (unlikely) or the agents of the Shadow (more likely). If it is a Shadow self for your hero, consider having him fall off some wagon or nearly falling off. He could be so shaken about this loss of Ordinary World that he reverts to some earlier bad habit.

One common character here is the Threshold Guardian who challenges the Hero. The Hero must pass this antagonistic character before he can leave the Ordinary World. Luke Skywalker gets in a fight with the alien in the cantina. Shrek has to defeat the knights in the arena. This is most often a mental or physical challenge. Think of it as tryouts for your Hero. He has to prove himself worthy of the journey.

Looking at the Star Wars movies can show you how the Hero's Journey can move through each individual story as well as the overarching trilogy. Don't use the idea of the Hero's Journey to create fences. Use it to expand your horizons of your story. This is about structure not "have to" rules. If every architect saw the four walls, roof and floor of a building in the same way, we wouldn't have English cottages or Victorian Painted Ladies, would we?

This card is also known as the First Threshold because there will be another point where the Hero has to make this kind of story-altering crossing. Here is the moment where the story takes off. The adventure has begun so I hope everyone is on board! This Millennium Falcon can't turn back now. Our Hero is now totally committed to this journey.

"The adventure is always and everywhere a passage

beyond the veil of the known into the unknown; the powers that watch at the boundary are dangerous; to deal with them is risky; yet for anyone with competence and courage the danger fades." (J Campbell)

Be careful, Luke! We are about to enter a realm where the rules and limits are unknown. Danger could be around the corner. Still our Hero knows he has to go forward.

Shuffle and cut and pull a card. What is your Hero's Threshold that must be crossed? SOUND THE CHARGE! Now it is time to write. You might use this formula as a leaping off point.

CROSSING THE THRESHOLD SPREAD

1. Hold the card that you drew for your Crossing the Threshold out.
2. Please note that you will be leaving all of the cards for the main Hero's Journey out and shuffling the rest back in if you choose to do these spreads.
3. Shuffle the deck at least 3-5 times.
4. Cut the deck into three piles.
5. Restack them so that the last cut is on top.
6. Draw two cards.
7. Lay the first one facedown to the left of the Crossing the Threshold.
8. Lay the second one facedown to the right of the Crossing the Threshold World.

Card One
Crossing the Threshold Card
Card Two

Card One (to the left) shows us the price your Hero faces if he crosses. This is who or what could be lost if he does cross. This is a big piece for your story because this can't be redeemed. Once he's made this choice, he can't backtrack. Once Arthur pulls the sword out of the stone, it cannot be put back in.

Card Two (to the right) represents the most compelling reason for crossing the Threshold. This is who or what could be lost if he doesn't cross. These cards truly represent the quintessential rock and hard place. If Arthur doesn't pull the sword out of that stone, Britain could be lost forever. He has to sacrifice his place in the world as just a young son or sacrifice the entire kingdom.

STORY TEMPLATE:

My hero, (name), started out in a world represented by (card). Now he has been called to adventure by (the card). But he refuses because (what reason does the card suggest?) The worst thing that could happen if he goes is (something from the card). His Mentor (card) taught him (card lesson) which made him realize (what does this card tell you about why he must Cross The Threshold).

Keep in mind that this is about getting the journey in place. You don't need to have a fully fleshed out story at this point. We are plotting. You can even do this as an outline if you prefer that method.

As always, please give yourself permission to wander around. If Lewis and Clark had stuck to the known routes, think of what would have been left undiscovered. Complete this part before moving on to the next lesson.

EXAMPLE:

Micah's moment of Crossing the Threshold was shown by the card Judgment. He is being held up to a standard he isn't aware of. His need to help Olivia forces him to ignore his own desire to not be Alpha. You see a large part of Micah's refusal revolves around him not wanting to be responsible for those who see him as their Alpha.

QUOTE

"Don't tell me the moon is shining; show me the glint of light on broken glass."
-- Anton Chekov

JOURNAL PROMPT

Write five sentences. Each one should use one of the five senses to describe light.

Write with joy, y'all. Show, don't tell. One of the things every beginning writer hears. One tip I have is to layer at least two senses into any description. Make your reader feel, hear, taste, smell, see what your hero is doing.

Chapter Seven
Act II

Tests, Allies + Enemies

No matter how many schools he has been through, he's a freshman all over again in this new world.
-- Christopher Vogler

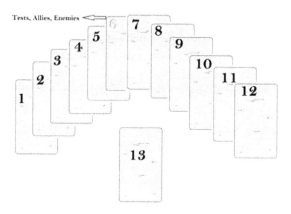

First day at the new school is always a bear. You don't know anyone. You don't know the rules. You don't know what the others already know. It's time for your Hero to learn. Sometimes this will be PhD books at the school of hard knocks.

The Hero must learn who can be trusted here. He will face tests that will try his will, his strength and, quite possibly, his patience. He must begin the task of facing his fears. We are talking the deep, dark, stuffed-in-a-box-shoved-under-the-bed fears. Even when he refused the call and hesitated on the threshold, all he did was acknowledge his fears. He might have superficially addressed them, but this is the point where he must go toe-to-toe with those terrors.

Consider that once he's crossed the threshold, everything is different. What he knew has now changed. The rhythm of his Ordinary World has completely warped. He is a fish out of water here. Don't give him too much water--just enough to survive. He needs to struggle to be interesting.

Here your reader will learn even more about your hero. As he faces the new rules and structures, he will reveal who he was. You can do some back-story extrapolation here. Always keep your reader in mind. If you were at a cocktail party, at what point would their eyes glaze over with boredom? Avoid that point. Leave them wanting more.

Tests reveal him, but who he chooses as friends shed a whole new light. Does a lonely orphan find a best friend who comes complete with a large, noisy family? Think of how Harry Potter was enveloped by the Weasley family. Or does your loner connect with a large group like The Hobbit's hero Bilbo Baggins when he meets the thirteen dwarves? What do his friends tell your reader about him? Harry Potter faced many tests, but the theme was the same in each of them. Would he allow evil to overcome the good in him? Talk about the battle between good and evil, right? How much more powerful was that because it was inside Harry as well as externally visible? These are key ingredients in this stage of your Hero's Journey. Also, remember that this is not static. Tests, Allies and Enemies are continual in your story.

Never forget that Allies can turn into Enemies. Or better yet, vice versa. You do have to be cautious. If you have made your Hero's enemy someone who makes Darth Vader look like a librarian, then you may lose your readers if he suddenly turns into the new sidekick. Allies are the sidekicks but also the parental figure or beauty shop owner. In Steel Magnolias, Truvy Jones is M'Lynn's very unlikely ally in that M'Lynn is an upper-class woman while Truvy is definitely from a lower social circle. The Allies in your story can be used for comparison and for contrast. Donkey is a great example of an Ally because he makes Shrek look good but also shows Shrek's many flaws. A flawless Hero is a boring character.

Enemies serve some of the same functions as the Friends. They are there to show you more about the hero. Think of both Enemies and Friends as mirrors. Your hero is reflected in how he interacts with them. If the Enemy kicks a puppy, your hero's response discloses more. Perhaps his own puppy was kicked by a childhood bully only the Hero didn't fight back then. What if an Enemy turns into an Ally? Can your Hero really trust them? In Gail Carriger's Parasol Protectorate, Geneviève Lefoux is a very gray character throughout the book. The main character wants to trust her but never feels that she can.

This lends a delicious tension to the entire story arc of those five books.

Friends and Enemies bring Tests. The very moral fiber of your Hero is called into question. His weaknesses are as important as his strengths. Who can forget Indiana Jones' initial reaction to the snake on the plane and the subsequent scene when he is lowered into the dig site where he finds the path to the Arc of the Holy Covenant in a massive pile of snakes? Luke's testing is ongoing. A first test comes in the Cantina when he is thrust into the world of alien creatures and manners. At each step, his tests are about how he sees himself through the filter of these new worlds. Think small town boy meets a very strange, very big city.

The Hero will need to get ready for the bigger Ordeal coming up (think facing the dragon bigger Ordeal). Here is the Hero sharpening his proverbial sword. He is taking what the Mentor taught him and moving further into his training. The Mentor could show up again at this point for another swift kick in the pants. Or a lesson learned from the Mentor could be used to save the Hero or one of his new-found friends. If the friend isn't new to the Hero, that is okay as well. Samwise was already a friend of Frodo but the friendship deepened for both of them throughout that trilogy. Also, don't disregard that other characters have their own journeys to make. This will add layers to your book.

In the Tarot, I would choose the High Priestess (HPS) for this position although others have put the Hermit in this spot. I choose the HPS because she is another aspect of the Mentor. Also, she represents Mystery (yes, with a capital M). She can be the gateway to the next level in terms of the tests your

Hero must face. The dark and light pillars behind her can be Friends and Enemies.

Traditionally this card is about learning what is within you. There is a phrase from The Charge of the Goddess that says, "And you who seek to know Me, know that the seeking and yearning will avail you not, unless you know the Mystery: for if that which you seek, you find not within yourself, you will never find it without."

These words are perfect for this stage of Tests, Allies and Enemies. The answers to "Friend or foe?" must come from within. Your Hero must pass the tests of his journey by listening to himself (or judging if the advice he is given is worth following.) The High Priestess has the knowledge but doesn't just drop it in his lap. Your Hero has to make the choice. He has to choose between the two pillars every time he makes a decision. All of this must come from within him. Even if you've given him the biggest, baddest sword along with the roughest, toughest, merriest band of followers the world has ever seen, it all boils down to the choices your Hero makes.

Reflect on the idea that this could be seen as a type of Initiation where the Hero has to pass certain tests in order to prove his commitment to the Journey. Even his friends may doubt his investment so some of the tests may come from them--even jokingly. Again, let me reiterate the fact that all good stories have a Hero's Journey. Your book can be a lighthearted romp through the fashion district of Milan or a death-defying, bullet-dodging dash across Manhattan. Both will have these elements if you want to offer a truly well-written story.

One other thing Friends do is serve as sounding

boards. Here is another good device for getting back-story out about your character. When your Hero is facing the tests, you can show his misgivings in his conversations with those he trusts. In the first Shrek movie, the Princess tells Donkey about her fears. You learn more about Fiona's back story here. Of course, Shrek overhears then misinterprets which creates his Big Black Moment. You can also see how Donkey serves as Ally in both Fiona's and Shrek's Hero's journey. Remember that all major characters need to have this journey. Minor characters such as Donkey do not need a full journey, but even a minor character will hit some of the steps.

Speaking of steps, this part of the Hero's Journey is less of a step and more of an on-going thing. He will be separated from his friends at some point. He will be confronted by his enemies or his fears. Throughout the story, he will be tested. This is not a one scene part of the story. I like to focus on this when I go back through my rough draft. Have I tested my character enough? Is he going to be bullet-proof when he has to face the Shadow? Can my version of Indiana Jones survive Samuel L. Jackson's snakes on that plane?

Enemies can be confronted here as well as Allies found so don't forget that. If you draw one card, that card will point out what is most important for your Hero's journey at this point. There is also the idea that the Hero is FORCED to make choices here as to who are his allies and who are his enemies.

See this as a series of trials where the Hero learns a bit more about the people around him. This can be a negotiation at the boardroom or a foray into enemy territory.

"...the process of dissolving, transcending, or

transmuting the infantile images of our personal past...Can the ego put itself to death?" ~ Joseph Campbell

For this step, I recommend pulling three cards. Let the first be the Test card. The second will be for Allies which leaves Enemies for the third. You can pull just one if you prefer, but for me, I need the individual information for each of these three components. This is more involved. You may wish to draw one and write about it before moving on to the next. You can use this template for your next part of this hero's journey.

TESTS, ALLIES and ENEMIES SPREAD

1. Hold the cards that you drew for your Test, Allies and Enemies out.
2. Please note that you will be leaving all of the cards for the main Hero's Journey out and shuffling the rest back in if you choose to do these spreads.
3. Shuffle the deck at least 3-5 times.
4. Cut the deck into three piles.
5. Restack them so that the last cut is on top.
6. Draw three cards.
7. Lay the first one facedown under the Test card.
8. Lay the second one facedown under the Enemies card.
9. Lay the third one face down under the Allies card.

Card One represents the most important thing your Hero learns from the tests throughout the book. This will be the thing that is reemphasized through the Journey. This is the lesson of the testing or the reason for the testing. If the Ace of Cups showed up here, I might divine that my Hero's test would be about who to love and how to show that love.

Card Two represents the most important Ally in your Hero's world. If this is a romance, this doesn't have to be the love interest. It could be the sidekick/best friend. Remember that the Ally is there to help your Hero. Even if you are using the Ally who turns into an Enemy, they are still helping the Hero by showing the Hero who he can really trust.

Card Three shows what motivates his enemies against him. This may be something about the Hero or it could be something about the Enemy. It is up to you as the writer to divine, then assign and refine. In Dorothy's case in the Wizard of Oz, the witch wanted her ruby slippers. For Shrek, the king wanted Fiona. It is often something the Hero has that the Enemy wants. When the Enemy is not cognizant (such as the weather in the Perfect Storm), then the Enemy wants the Hero's life (or equally important thing.)

STORY TEMPLATE:

My hero, (name), started out in a world represented by (card). Now he has been called to adventure by (the card). But he refuses because (what reason does the card suggest?) The worst thing that could happen if he goes is (something from the card). His Mentor (card) taught him (card lesson) which made him realize (why he had to Cross The Threshold). Now my hero is going to be tested by (Test card). I see (symbols/images) which makes me think about (either the part of your hero about to be tested or what the test is going to be). His Allies are represented by (Allies card). I see his friend(s) as (characteristics from the card.) His Enemies are represented by (Enemies card). I see his enemy as (characteristics from the card.)

You can do some characterization of friends and enemies here as well. You might pull the court cards from the four suits and draw a card for each enemy and each friend. Detail what you see in the cards. You can even use the physical attributes if you like.

The important part of this lesson is to remember that all three are tests for your Hero. Complete this part before moving on to the next lesson.

EXAMPLE:

For Tests, Enemies and Allies, Micah's test is represented by the King of Cups. He has to have his emotional involvement tested. His enemies are the Compound Pack who show up as the Five of Wands which carries a meaning of jockeying for position and trying to win at any costs. His Allies were the Six of Coins which represented the generosity of his friends Gareth, Tony and Pete.

QUOTE

Literature is strewn with the wreckage of men who have minded beyond reason the opinions of others.
-- Virginia Woolf

JOURNAL PROMPT

Who has told you can't write? Why do you still write? What do you know that they don't know? Why does their opinion matter to you?

Write with joy, y'all. Critique happens. There will always be someone who thinks they can write a better book. Let them. Don't let them into your head. Keep your personal sanctuary critic-free.

Chapter Eight

Approach The Inmost Cave

Don't let your fear paralyze you. Prepare yourself not only technically, but also emotionally.
-- Bob Weinstein

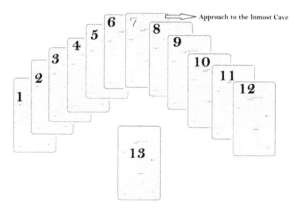

The seventh card in this spread is the Approach to the Inmost Cave or the Supreme Ordeal is another name. As Writers, we will recognize this as one of the Black

Moments of the book. Here our Hero must review his plans and upcoming attacks. He may launch a reconnoitering mission as well. Are you prepared? Really Big Bad Thing is coming up soon. You've just found the last note that tells you where the bomb is and the clock is now doing that countdown we all love to hate.

Please note this step is not about who or what is in the cave. It's about the road there. Do watch out for potholes, please. This card could signal the old gang getting back together despite all that's torn them apart. At this point, the Big Bad Thing is bigger than issues between them. This is a good time for tension building. Consider how Shrek and Donkey fight right before the big "storm the castle" scene. They are approaching the inmost cave. Or Dorothy is captured by the Wicked Witch then forced to see how her Aunt Em is ill from grieving for her.

If you have lovers in your story, here is a traditional place to have them promise to love one another or at least admit there's something there. But now is not the time to explore that. You reveal it to your readers then make them wait for it. Because, you know, there's the Big Bad Thing down the road. And there's nothing sillier than a sex scene right before the show down with the villain. Talk about being caught with your pants down!

Your Hero has to plot and plan for the inevitable confrontation. Even in a romance with no danger or Darth Vader in the dungeon, he must address how he is going to get the girl. The danger could be that she may not love him or want him. Let's suppose he's told her that he loves her, but she hasn't indicated that she reciprocates those feelings. In a romance, the Cave (also known as the Ordeal) is the Big Black Moment so this is preparation for that. You want him (or her) to lay their soul bare to someone only to have that someone not respond for whatever reason you give them. For instance, Fiona's Big Black Moment comes when she bares her soul but Shrek acts as if he doesn't care. She decides to marry Lord Farquaad even though she is in love with Shrek. But her Approach is her telling Donkey her secret. Shrek's Approach is overhearing the conversation and misinterpreting what he hears. Notice that their journeys are not on the same timeline.

Now, S, if your story is more action than romance, now would be a good time to check how many bullets are in the gun. Joseph Campbell discusses how this is where the hero enters another world. Think Orpheus descending to save his wife from the underworld. Consider that your hero has gotten so used to the new world that it has now become the Ordinary World.

This is his build-up to crossing another threshold only he won't have the luxury of a mentor here. He must take the lessons he's learned and use them. Many stories have a physical representation of this cave that must be entered. For Dorothy, it's the witch's castle. For Shrek, it's the castle where Fiona is about to say, "I do." For Jake Sully, it's the loss of the support of the N'avi-or more importantly, the loss of Neyteri's trust. Vogler discusses this moment as a "disheartening setback" or "dramatic complication."

How your hero handles this complication is up to you. It's your voice that sets the tone. Shall we tell jokes, trade kisses or plan for the coming war? There is a palpable tension here because we are heading into the dénouement of the book. Use this card to see what you need to emphasize at this point of the book.

The Tarot card I would associate with this position would be Justice (which is what others also have put here.) This is where the Hero must make a leap of faith that will take him to the next level. He's possibly hit some setbacks which require him to review his methods. He may need a new idea that he can only get as he approaches the Inmost Cave or Supreme Ordeal.

Justice is often depicted as a blindfolded individual (often a woman) who holds up a scale. The idea is that what you've done in your life has led you to this point. No one but your hero is responsible for his being just outside this cave. It is time for him to take personal responsibility for his life.

Don't skimp on this step. Justice is about coming to terms with your conscience. A favorite deck of mine depicts Justice as the Egyptian Goddess Ma'at. She holds a scale in one hand. On that scale she will place your heart. The other side will hold a red feather. It is said that if your heart is not lighter than that red feather, your soul will be eaten instead of moving on to the next level. Your Hero should have the sense that he could not only lose everything-he could lose himself.

Here is where you want to layer in a heightened sense of "what's going to happen next?" This is where you can begin preparing your reader with some foreshadowing. Hopefully you have been foreshadowing a bit already.

You want to set your readers up. For the next screaming ride down the rollercoaster hill that is. Do this part well and you will have your readers eating out of the palm of your hand. Build your Hero up then tear him down. Your Hero must show his willingness to change even if that means his own death or the loss of the love of his life. He must recognize what he was and what he is becoming. This is another verification that he cannot go back to the person he was in the Ordinary World.

One thing to consider is your hero's head space. As he is walking down that corridor towards the door where he knows his father waits, what is he thinking about? How does he carry himself? You bet that Luke wasn't thinking about pod racing or Womp rat shooting. He's weighing out the cost of killing his own parent. Twist your hero up. Tear him apart like the Scarecrow getting stripped of his straw. Your hero can't break here but you can certainly show how much is at stake. And the stakes must be higher than any other point in your story.

Often the hero has to revisit old angst. This can go back to that first Refusal. He could bring up the same worries and misgivings he had then. Have him look back at why he first didn't want to do this journey. Maybe he could have an "I told you so" moment with himself. He knows that the path in front of him is the worst bit. This is St. George sitting on his horse looking at the dragon's cave. It's why he crossed that threshold in the first place. Is he ready?

"The Hero must make the preparations needed to approach the Inmost Cave that leads to the Journey's heart, or central Ordeal. Maps may be reviewed, attacks planned, a reconnaissance launched, and possibly the enemy forces whittled down before the Hero can face his greatest fear, or the supreme danger lurking in the Special World." Vogler

To paraphrase Bob Weinstein, "Don't let your hero's fear paralyze him."

For this part, lay the preceding cards out. There are twelve spots that create an arch. This is the top of the arch along with the spot before. The next five spots will begin the downward leg of the journey.

Shuffle and cut the cards as you have been. Review what's come before then turn over the top card. What do you see in this card? What is your immediate visceral reaction? Write about that. Let this be the emotion your Hero has as he has to traverse this last corridor to the cave. This is another time to stop and review symbols. Has anything repeated? A color? A bird? If so, what does that symbol mean to you? As a reminder, this is to help you learn to use the Tarot cards as creativity tools so your take on the card is more important than any traditional meaning.

As before, open your journal to record what you see here.

APPROACH TO THE INMOST CAVE SPREAD

1. Hold the card that you drew for your Approach to the Inmost Cave out.
2. Please note that you will be leaving all of the cards for the main Hero's Journey out and shuffling the rest back in if you choose to do these spreads.
3. Shuffle the deck at least 3-5 times.
4. Cut the deck into three piles.
5. Restack them so that the last cut is on top.
6. Draw two cards.

7. Lay the first one facedown to the left of the Approach card.
8. Lay the second one facedown to the right of the Approach Card.

Card One
Approach Card
Card Two

Card One (To the left) is leap of faith your Hero must take in order to approach this ordeal. This can be something he has to believe in or just trust in. Shrek had to navigate past his feelings of betrayal.

Card Two (To the right) represents the old angst that your Hero revisits. How does this card connect with card three, the Refusal? Jake Sully had to face the idea that he had betrayed the humans by supporting the N'avi.

STORY TEMPLATE:

My hero, (name), started out in a world represented by (card). Now he has been called to adventure by (the card). But he refuses because (what reason does the card suggest?) The worst thing that could happen if he goes is (something from the card). His Mentor (card) taught him (card lesson) which made him realize (why he had to Cross The Threshold). Now my hero is going to be tested by (Test card). His Allies are represented by (Allies card). His Enemies are represented by (Enemies card).

My hero must face (Inmost Cave Card) which represents his biggest loss (what is that loss?)

EXAMPLE:

For the Approach card, the King of Coins stands guard. He represents all the people who depend upon Micah. Micah has to grapple with the idea that he is that important to others.

QUOTE

Anyone who tells you there's a "right" way to write is a lying bitch.
-- Nora Roberts as seen on Angela James' Tumblr

JOURNAL PROMPT

What are your rules for writing? Write about some of the rules you've heard that you just have to break!

Write with joy, y'all. There are as many rules about writing as there are about which fork to use for your salad. Learn them. Then use the ones that work for you. Here's a hint. There is no Writing Police force out to get you! Write what you love and tell a good story.

Chapter Nine

The Ordeal

The artist is extremely lucky who is presented with the worst possible ordeal which will not actually kill him. At that point, he's in business.
-- John Berryman

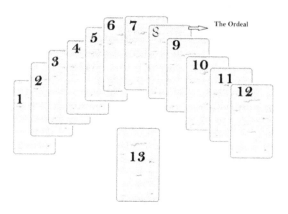

Please cue the Death March music. No. That's a little too peppy--too bright. Let's go for Night on Bald Mountain by Modes Mussorgsky. Ah yes, that's better.

After all, we need mood music for this eighth step on our Hero's Journey. We've twisted our Hero up into knots with the Approach to the Inmost Cave. He's confessed his love, his fallibilities, even his fears. He's sharpened all his weapons both physical and metaphorical. He's studied the maps and conferred with his friends.

Now he has to leave everyone and everything behind. He must enter the Cave where he knows his final doom could be waiting. Jake Sully has to realize that all is lost. Grace is dying. The Home Tree is down. Neytiri loves him no more. Dorothy has to understand that her Aunt is ill because she ran away. Remember we aren't calling this step "the kind of bad thing that sort of happens." We aren't labeling it "the icky thing we can probably avoid." No. This is a big fat hairy ORDEAL. And your Hero must face it alone.

This is the central life-or-death crisis of your story. There may have been battles and bad things before this, but this is the championship game. The Hero has to look into a mirror and face the GREATEST, MOST DIFFICULT, REALLY SCARY MOMENT of his life (to this point-grin.) Everything the Hero has worked so hard for could go up in smoke at this point. It is truly one of the most crucial moments of any good book.

Think of it in terms of death and resurrection. The Hero hits bottom and can only go up from there. What happens here will transform your character. This experience recreates or confirms your Hero. Rebirth is a word used a lot at this stage of the journey. You can see the obvious parallel to the journey of Christ here. Your Hero is not getting nailed to a cross most likely, but he is going to suffer. Don't skimp here. Your readers earned this part. They want you to make them cry. They want to hurt for your Hero as he tells his love goodbye forever.

There's really only one Tarot card for this part and it's our friend the Death card. Death is about change. Uncomfortable, hard, irreversible change which the Hero must face. This change, this Ordeal, is unavoidable. He goes into the Cave with the full knowledge that he only thought he'd been changed before. He understands that this could be the end of everything and everyone he holds dear. If your Hero isn't scared here, he isn't paying attention.

To be transformed is terrifying. Your Hero has no control over what the transformation will be. He could be changed into something that no one will want. Maybe this battle will change him into his father (Luke Skywalker/Darth Vader). Can he face what must be faced? Well, he doesn't really have a choice here, does he? Remember, you've made it so he can't go back to his Ordinary World. Frodo must get past Shelob (Lord of the Rings).

Think of what your Hero has to lose here. Add it all up and put it in one fragile basket along with some precious things of other characters just to make it really scary. Not only is he doing this for himself--he has others depending on him. Shrek now understands the Fairytale creatures in his swamp so he knows that his failure also hurts them. He's become responsible for the well-being of others.

What this means is that your Hero will most likely have to sacrifice something huge. Often in a romance, this is the spot where the character bravely gives up their lover in order to save them or the town or the cat. (Apologies to the "save the cat" fans... I'm not dissing that!) Your Hero may realize that in order for someone else to succeed, he must lose. Think of the Beast who lets Beauty go home even though he knows he will die without her.

The Hero has to let go of old thought patterns, outdated ways of seeing themselves and limiting beliefs. This is Christ in the garden at Gethsemane where he knew what was coming and knew that he had to do this in order to save the world. (Yes, I do see the story of the Christ as a Hero's Journey. I do not mean anything negative by that! I think the Christ avatar is one of the most amazing stories of our time of a truly amazing person who transcends human knowledge.)

Death of the old self is what this is about. On some more tragic, dark journeys, the Hero will have to sacrifice others in order to make this transformation. Think of the final battle on the Death Star where Red Leader 1 is killed (I still cry at that part.) The Ally will prove useful here as well in terms of helping the Hero through this transformation. The Ally is also the witness. This is the character that takes back the news that the Hero has died/failed.

Again, you need to be thinking in terms of your reader here. Make them believe your hero has crashed and burned. Rope them into the knowledge that no one can escape the situation he is in. The Approach to the Cave is a type of black moment in that he had to face fears. This, however, is the essential black moment because the Hero goes in knowing he will lose everything and/or everyone he ever cared about. His life being in jeopardy should play second fiddle to what he can lose.

The battle with Gilgamesh is a classic Ordeal. Frodo at Mount Doom struggling with Gollum and

Samwise is another. Your reader is standing outside breathlessly waiting to see if the Hero will survive this or be damaged beyond all hope of repair.

It's critical to the health and well-being of a truly good story. Am I getting that across? This is a part of the magic that will make the Hero larger-than-life but also one with the audience. The audience has bought into the story so that this point brings them down--even makes them cry--then replaces that emotion with joy when your Hero returns.

A great analogy is a rollercoaster ride. This is the careening, screaming dive from the very top of the hill. If you like roller coasters (and personally I hate 'em), you have experienced that adrenaline rush of "Sweet! I survived that. Let's go!" If you have ever belonged to a secret society like a fraternity or sorority, you have gone through some rite of passage that probably created this thrill of fear. It's a bond. It is said that you are never more alive than when you think you're going to die. This is similar to the "nothing to lose" attitude of some warriors plunging into battle. Or, as Crazy Horse supposedly said, "It's a good day to die."

After this Ordeal, the Hero is born into their new life with new responsibilities more than likely. Still, as John Berryman said, "The artist is extremely lucky who is presented with the worst possible ordeal which will not actually kill him. At that point, he's in business." This isn't the end of his journey. There are four more stages left.

Shuffle the cards while you focus on the journey of the Hero. Consider the last seven cards. Review them as you shuffle. Cut the cards into three piles and restack them. Now take that top card and write it out.

How does this card show fear, despair, loss? Maybe it shows what he fears losing? Perhaps the image shows the actual villain he must finally face here. Focus on what images pop out at you. How would the Hero feel if he lost his dog, his girl, his best friend, the planet?

ORDEAL SPREAD

1. Hold the card that you drew for your Ordeal out.
2. Please note that you will be leaving all of the cards for the main Hero's Journey out and shuffling the rest back in if you choose to do these spreads.
3. Shuffle the deck at least 3-5 times.
4. Cut the deck into three piles.
5. Restack them so that the last cut is on top.
6. Draw two cards.
7. Lay the first one facedown to the left of the Ordeal card.
8. Lay the second one facedown to the right of the Ordeal Card.

Card One
Ordeal Card
Card Two

Card One (To the left) will be the lowest point your Hero hits. This is the emotional rock-bottom card. Don't be afraid to dig the knife in. This must hurt. You want to make your reader be so emotionally involved with this Hero that they will cry.

Card Two (To the right) represents the thing your

Hero will lose (or think he loses) during the Ordeal. This should make your Hero want to do whatever it takes to not lose this. If it is a lover, make him realize he has to change some core value. If it is a life, make him offer up his as a substitute. This is the true moment of heroic sacrifice.

STORY TEMPLATE:

My hero, (name), started out in a world represented by (card). Now he has been called to adventure by (the card). But he refuses because (what reason does the card suggest?) The worst thing that could happen if he goes is (something from the card). His Mentor (card) taught him (card lesson) which made him realize (why he had to Cross The Threshold). Now my hero is going to be tested by (Test card). His Allies are represented by (Allies card). His Enemies are represented by (Enemies card). My hero faced the (Inmost Cave Card).

His Ordeal is that he has to face (Ordeal Card) in order to defeat (villain or stands as the villain.)

EXAMPLE:

For the Ordeal card, the Knight of Cups is here. This is Micah's internal struggle with himself. He knows he has to unlock his own emotions but how to do that? This is his battle with his love for the female shifter who has left him. He also must acknowledge that he is an Alpha to his Pack. He is forced here to choose between Pack and Love. He has to step up to the plate.

QUOTE

It is the writer who might catch the imagination of young people, and plant a seed that will flower and come to fruition.
-- Isaac Asimov

JOURNAL PROMPT

What did you read about when you were younger that is now real?

Write with joy, y'all. Think of everything that used to be fictional that is now real. Cars that talk to you. Wrist communicators. Computers that fit in your purse. What imaginary thing or idea is now real?

Chapter Ten

Reward

For them to perceive the advantage of defeating the enemy, they must also have their rewards.
-- Sun Tzu

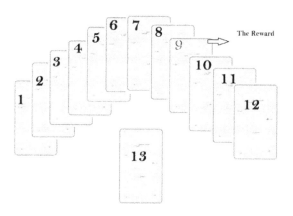

Sun Tzu brings up a good point. Your hero has struggled so hard. Here is the moment he's worked for all this time. Step nine in the Hero's Journey is the

Reward which is also known as Seizing the Sword. The Hero has been through hell. He's answered the call even though he didn't want to. His mentor kicked his butt while forcing him to see that he did have what it takes. He's taken that step that means he can never be the same person he was before. He's passed tests and made friends and identified enemies. He's walked right up to Death. He's defeated his own biggest fear. He needs a cookie.

During that intense struggle in the last step, your Hero should have learned something about himself. This should be both an inner and an outer revelation. This is the point where your hero learns he's the son of a God or his father is the *über* villain. He has to deal with this on some level. Your reader and your Hero know that there is more to him. He underestimated his own strengths. He also may see through any Shadow figures still masquerading as Allies.

You might consider that he could get a "big head". By this I mean your Hero may see himself as invincible with no limits on his behavior. Sometimes he walks away from the battle of the Ordeal marked by the battle. He carries some small piece of what he defeated. This taint can affect him on the next step of his journey. He could go from rational thinker to a "shoot first, ask questions later" type. It's also a good time to have him heave a sigh of relief that it's all over--even though it's not. It makes for a more powerful impact when the villain rises up to smack your Hero down again. If he believes himself to be ten foot tall and bulletproof.

In romances, this is very often where the hero and heroine pledge themselves to the partnership and one another. Consider the heroine as the physical representation of what the Hero's been going for. She is his reward. That's a bit sexist if you don't realize that he is her reward as well. Remember that in a novel with more than one lead character, both characters have their own Hero's Journeys to take. The Reward is where they merge those journeys even if the previous steps have looked different.

Consider this step a respite for both hero and reader. It is time to take a step back. Time to breathe after all that focus that lead up to the Ordeal is needed for everyone. Let your Hero had his moment to enjoy his prize but also to reflect on what he learned. You can use this step to foreshadow challenges that the Hero will face on the Road Back. For the sake of your readers, your Hero needs this moment to enjoy what he fought for. We all know that Michael (Halloween) is going to show up again. This is just letting us all catch our breaths before we head down that last rollercoaster hill.

Pay attention to that idea of letting your reader catch their breath. Pacing is extremely important no matter what type of story you are telling. Even a good comedian gives you time before the punch line. This is, as kids say today, the time to chillax, dude. Kicking back with a beer around the fire with his Allies, the Hero needs this time to reflect on where he's been. He may realize that this moment that he is simply not the person he was in his Ordinary World.

You can see this in Wizard of Oz when Dorothy returns the witch's broom only to find that the man behind the curtain is a charlatan. Luke finds out his father is the live villain not the dead hero he thought. Vogler refers to this as a moment of divine recognition.

The key for Dorothy on her Road Back will be to realize that she must be her own vehicle. In other words, Dorothy Gayle has to accept herself and her Ordinary World in order to return.

Something to consider here is the concept of Explicit Recognition that Campbell discusses. This is where the Hero cannot avoid facing the fact that there is something different about him. A favorite old movie of mine is Sgt. York. In this movie, a pacifist is thrown into a war situation. He becomes a decorated war hero when he saves his platoon. That is his moment of Explicit Recognition--he cannot deny that his skill as a sharpshooter (used for hunting only) has saved not only his life, but many others. Other moments of Explicit Recognition can be seen in Avatar when Colonel Miles Quaritch, asks Jake Sully, "Hey Sully...how does it feel to betray your own race? You think you're one of them? Time to wake up!" Sully's response is his moment of Explicit Recognition. He lays his ears back, lashes his tail and snarls. He sees himself as Na'vi rather than human.

Remember. Your Hero has survived the Ordeal so give him something really good. This is not the time for the cheap lollipop dentists used to offer. What we need here is double-layered dark chocolate cake with raspberry filling. You cannot stint on the reward or your readers will be disappointed.

How the Hero gets the Reward is important. If he stole it, there may be some lingering doubts. Does he deserve this Reward? He could decide that he does deserve it because of the Tests he passed and the Ordeals he went though. But even a Hero, if a thief, must pay for the crime. This will be seen on the Road

Back. The Shadow forces will come after him to reclaim it. The Shadow forces cannot allow the Reward or Elixir to be seen in the Ordinary World. Efforts to stop the Hero are ramping up. While the Hero takes his well-deserved break, the bad guys are going double or nothing to stop him.

For the fifth step, Crossing the Threshold, your Hero had to face down the Threshold Guardians. At this point, part of his reward may be those same characters joining his side or lending him their aid. His own Allies will also see him in a new light at this point. There may be a subtle shift that moves him from new kid to respected compatriot. This is where Luke is saluted by the other rebels. He's one of them now.

A good card for this is the card of ultimate balance-- Temperance. This is the card that represents the reward you get for holding back. Think of it as the clearheaded morning after an evening where your friends overindulged and you limited yourself to two glasses of wine instead of four. Temperance is a card that often depicts a figure transforming energy. You will see fire flowing from one hand only to end up as water in the other. The idea here is that transformation is taking place.

Now the next question is how will your Hero handle this Reward? Will he run back to his room to eat the cake all by himself? Will he share the Elixir with others? This temptation here will show us what the Hero still needs to learn. Remember he is not out of the woods yet! There are still tasks to be completed. What he does here indicates how successful he will be on the road home.

This card can be connected back to card two to show how the Hero has grown on a spiritual level.

This is his reward for Answering the Call. What is special about this Reward? Has the Hero gained knowledge about himself or the mystery or the villain or the love interest? Does he have a physical object that he must carry back? Remember that whatever he has gained, the Shadow forces seek to take it back. And sometimes this is a reconciliation of a conflict such as Luke discovering Darth Vader is his father and might still have a glimmer of goodness in him.

REWARD SPREAD

1. Hold the card that you drew for your Reward out.
2. Please note that you will be leaving all of the cards for the main Hero's Journey out and shuffling the rest back in if you choose to do these spreads.
3. Shuffle the deck at least 3-5 times.
4. Cut the deck into three piles.
5. Restack them so that the last cut is on top.
6. Draw two cards.
7. Lay the first one facedown to the left of the Reward card.
8. Lay the second one facedown to the right of the Reward Card.

Card One
Reward Card
Card Two

Card One (To the left) is how the Hero gets the Reward. This will help you determine a way to access this Reward. Don't forget that the Reward is often stolen by the Hero. That creates a conflict in the Hero who is supposed to be good but has to do something bad to be good.

Card Two (To the right) shows what the Reward is. Remember that it is not always tangible so you may need to think outside of the box. What symbols are on this card that could be the actual Reward? A rabbit might symbolize fertility for instance.

STORY TEMPLATE:

My hero, (name), started out in a world represented by (card). Now he has been called to adventure by (the card). But he refuses because (what reason does the card suggest?) The worst thing that could happen if he goes is (something from the card). His Mentor (card) taught him (card lesson) which made him realize (why he had to Cross The Threshold). Now my hero is going to be tested by (Test card). His Allies are represented by (Allies card). His Enemies are represented by (Enemies card). My hero faced the (Inmost Cave Card). He faced his Ordeal which was (Ordeal Card).

Now his reward is (Reward card) which is (or symbolizes) the reason he crossed the threshold in the first place.

EXAMPLE:

The Reward card is the 10 of Cups which is the card of family and happily ever after. Micah's reward comes in finding all of his Pack and friends and Olivia waiting for him when he enters the courtroom sure that he will be labeled a lone wolf--a danger to his society. Everyone is there pulling for him.

Now is the time to shuffle that deck and draw that card. What Reward waits for your hero?

QUOTE

"When writing a novel a writer should create living people; people, not characters. A character is a caricature."
-- Ernest Hemingway

JOURNAL PROMPT

Who's the craziest character you know in real life? What makes them stand out in your mind?

Write with joy, y'all. Remember that characters are flawed if they are interesting. The perfect hero or heroine is boring. You need to give them a scar-- external or internal. Make them real, not perfect.

Chapter Eleven
Act III

The Road Back

The question isn't who is going to let me; it's who is going to stop me.
-- Ayn Rand, The Fountainhead

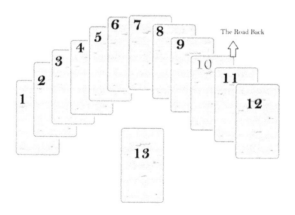

Now we open the third and final act. Your Hero cannot just lollygag about while patting himself on the back. He has to finish his journey. He has to remember why he crossed that First Threshold. At this stage, there is often a Second Refusal. Just like the Hero refused the Call to Adventure, he now doesn't want to go on. He knows he has to because he has to finish his journey.

However the Road Back is not necessarily a return to the Ordinary World. This is the final part of the initial Call to Action. He had to learn to believe in himself. That is part of the Reward. Now he has to complete the journey by carrying the Reward to those who need it. This marks the beginning of the third and final act of this story.

Your Hero must recommit. Not to the idea of being on the Journey, but to actually completing the Journey. Your Hero knows his role will change. He may not want this to happen. I mean think about it. He realized that he would be irrevocably changed if he accepted that Call to Adventure. He's received training from the Mentor that gave him knowledge/skills that had to have changed him. Now he must complete this task. What is left for him after that?

This card represents an Event (capital E). This moment will push the Hero back across the Threshold forcing him to action and once again upping the ante. This Event could be the Hero having to choose between his own heart and a higher cause. A time-honored version of this is the Beast sending Belle home even though he knows he will die. He chooses her happiness (higher cause) over his own heart. Luke had to get the Death Star plans back to the rebel base.

This can be the thing that galvanizes your hero to put aside any doubts or misgivings that he has. She must let the hero go. He must shoot his dog. He must take that last shot. There are so many climatic moments that we could look at. Take a moment to think of one of your favorite books or movies. Where is that Second Refusal that marks the Hero's stepping on to the Road Back?

One card some would put here is the Devil. I can see how that fits since the Devil represents temptation--the temptation to not go. The Devil works in that this is a can't-be-avoided encounter with the Shadow. The Hero has become a tool for the storyline here and his only job is to destroy the Shadow. Say good-bye, Death Star. Time to get blown to smithereens! Old patterns must go for both the Hero and his nemesis.

However, for me, this is a Tower moment. Tower moments are those unavoidable, messy moments where your Hero's life is upended. I think it takes this kind of upheaval to motivate your Hero to head back towards the Ordinary World. One Tarot reader once told me that she views the Tower as being built of lies we tell ourselves--which makes perfect sense to me when I think about my own Tower moments in life.

Consider the pain it will cause your Hero when he must face that fact that his own actions and choices have brought him to this moment. Make him own up to all he has done for maximum gut wrenching. He must review all that's led up to this moment. Once he realizes that he had to make the choices and pay the consequences, then he can begin to see how to negotiate the Road Back.

Because this is a spot where you ratchet the tension up, a case could also be made for the Hanged Man who represents not only being forced to wait, but also sacrifice. This card is the one that can call for you to have to give something up in order to get something. Remember this. It isn't something small. It's big. But even with the theme of sacrifice here, I would still go with the Tower as the card that best represents this turn to the Road Back. That's because Crossing the Second Threshold needs to be very powerful. You want your reader gasping in shock. The movement is swift with danger at every turn.

Perhaps what motivates your Hero forward is his own death/transformation. Maybe this is the thing that causes them to acknowledge their own role as sacrificial lamb. They know that their own death will let those who follow them live on in freedom. Consider Frodo in the final scene of the first movie in the Lord of the Rings trilogy. He is in a boat alone heading towards Mordor. Of course, Samwise joins him but this is a pivotal moment in that storyline.

I suggest that killing off your Hero is not the best way to go. I would hazard a guess that it is too risky in the book world to shatter your readers that way. Unless your Hero is a human who will be reborn as some immortal creature, killing him is a very bad idea. In Avatar this moment for Jake Sully would be where he goes after the Turok to become the Toruk Makto. He must lead his new people against his old people.

Whatever this Event is that ups the stakes and tension, it should bring the reader back to the Central Dramatic Question. This is a term used to describe the tension that your reader should maintain. It's not stated in the story so much as in the head of the reader. Will the Hero complete the task? Is he as evil as his father? Will she find true love?

This is a turning point in the book. Your story could change direction. Your Hero may lose the Elixir which creates a new level of anxiety as she chases the Shadow back. Here is where a Hero may have to give up the seemingly higher cause for the one of her heart. This Event can be either external (discovering a Doomsday Clock) or internal (the only way to make her happy is to let her marry the other guy). Whatever it is, it will be huge. One possibility is to upend the Hero. Make him seemingly lose everything here.

The Hero brings a new way of seeing things to this Road Back. It is what helps him to triumph over the Shadow. Think of it as his secret trump card--his new-found strength in self. He now sees himself in a new light. But also remember that he may have been tainted by Shadow during the Ordeal. Shadow is much closer during this part of the book as your Hero races to the end. Vogler points out that here is where your Hero once again acknowledges how he's changed. The old ways won't work now. He's got to try something else.

And think of the action you can have here. This is a great chase point in your story. Remember Elliott and E.T. as they lift off into the moonlight on the bike? That is this moment in their Hero's Journey. If you have bad guys, this is where they make another play for your Hero. The Shadow Forces CANNOT let that elixir back into the Ordinary World. The Hero HAS to get that elixir back. Quite often you have a time element here. Something or someone is going to go BOOM if the Hero doesn't get there by a certain moment.

If you don't have a villain, Shadow attacks can be the Hero's own insecurities. Perhaps his old fears or habits return threatening to take him under. Maybe a flaw that she thought she'd overcome shows back up.

It could be that one of the minor characters dies at this point. This heightens the emotional investment for the reader as well as possibly being the Event itself.

The Hero chooses to head back to the Ordinary World. He has to take all that he has learned and make it mesh with who he was and who he is now. He could have new guides or old ones show up here to help him back to the Ordinary World. One essay I read said, "The Hero has gained the wisdom to know how to ask for help." And that's a hard thing for any of us, isn't it?

Shanna Swendson suggests that this could be called the Approach to the Moment of Truth. I like this as a mirror to the Approach the Inmost Cave. This is an inescapable moment for your Hero. Some of his companions may not make it back. There is no going back. More importantly, there will be no more second chances. This is Luke's one shot at the one weakness on the Death Star. This is Dorothy's strength of belief that clicking her heels will get her home again. Will they make it?

Time to shuffle and cut and draw a card. What will your Hero's next step be? How will he approach The Road Back?

THE ROAD BACK SPREAD

1. Please note that you will be leaving all of the cards for the main Hero's Journey out and shuffling the rest back in if you choose to do these spreads.
2. Shuffle the deck at least 3-5 times.
3. Cut the deck into three piles.
4. Restack them so that the last cut is on top.
5. Draw two cards.

6. Lay the first one facedown to the left of the Road Back card.
7. Lay the second one facedown to the right of the Road Back Card.

Card One
The Road Back Card
Card Two

Card One (To the left) is what motivates your Hero to return. This is what kicks him over this next threshold. Jake realizes that he has to lead the N'avi to battle.

Card Two (To the right) shows how the Shadow will attack your Hero. This is his vulnerability--the soft spot in his armor. Colonel Quaritch has pinned Neytiri. He is going for the killing blow when Jake rallies to attack him.

STORY TEMPLATE:

My hero, (name), started out in a world represented by (card). Now he has been called to adventure by (the card). But he refuses because (what reason does the card suggest?) The worst thing that could happen if he goes is (something from the card). His Mentor (card) taught him (card lesson) which made him realize (why he had to Cross The Threshold). Now my hero is going to be tested by (Test card). His Allies are represented by (Allies card). His Enemies are represented by (Enemies card). My hero faced the (Inmost Cave card). He faced his Ordeal which was (Ordeal card). He got his reward which was (Reward card.)

The Road Back is represented by this one story turning event (Road Back card.)

EXAMPLE:

In Changing Focus, Micah's return is marked by the Page of Coins. He returned to New Orleans where he received his Reward. Now he must get down to the business of being a Pack leader as well as a father and husband. He's got work to do says the Page of Coins.

QUOTE

I love deadlines. I like the whooshing sound they make as they fly by.
-- Douglas Adams

JOURNAL PROMPT

What deadlines do you have? Write down a deadline today. Challenge yourself to meet it whether it is 5 pages in two days or writing 30 minutes every day.

Write with joy, y'all. Deadlines are fictional unless there's an editor involved. But that doesn't mean you can't practice meeting a deadline. Why not challenge yourself? Count your words and set a goal for two days from now.

Chapter Twelve

Resurrection

The resurrection gives my life meaning and direction and the opportunity to start over no matter what my circumstances.
-- ~Robert Flatt

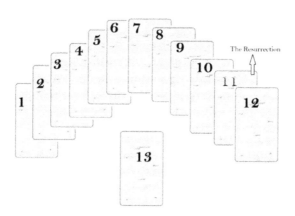

Step eleven in the Hero's Journey is a doozy. This, like the Ordeal, is a pivotal moment in your story. Your Hero has faced his Ordeal and survived. Now he must do it again. What makes this worse is he knows how hard it was last time. Here is his most dangerous meeting with death where death stands for all that he could lose if he screws this up.

Ever had your heart completely shattered and then faced the chance to love again? Remember how scary that was? Or been in a horrific car accident? How did it feel to get behind that wheel again? Some people never move past that Ordeal moment. They are stuck in a fear cage of their own making. This card is Resurrection.

Just like any resurrection, your Hero now faces his most terrifying moment. He must look Death in the eye. He could lose his love interest, his life, his self-respect--whatever is dearest to him could be gone in the blink of an eye. It could be more than one thing so don't rule out combo packages like his love dies and he is maimed for life. Think big and bad and scary. Here is where you as the writer must one-up yourself. This happens on the road back to the Ordinary World or at the moment he steps into the Ordinary World. Like the Threshold position, there is no going backwards. We are talking Big Black Moment here.

Every parting gives a foretaste of death; every coming together again a foretaste of the resurrection.
-- Arthur Schopenhauer

This card can represent either the plunge before the Resurrection or the purification after the Resurrection. What does your Hero fear losing the most? If you aren't sure, stop. This is important because without this--you just have a journey. You do not have a Hero's Journey. And all great stories have Hero's Journeys, right? You want this to be a great story so make it one by upping the ante here.

If you aren't sure what your Hero fears losing the most--that's important because this is a single thing that would devastate him if he lost this--you may want to pick up a full Tarot deck. Draw a card (after shuffling and cutting). I say a full deck because all of the cards need to come into play here. What if what he fears most is one of the cards you've already drawn? Don't you think that will give you a bit more insight into your Hero?

Consider that what he fears losing most may not be what he (or you) expects. Instead of the heroine, it could be his self-respect or his ability to play the violin. In romance it is often the other person, but what if it is a show-down between losing the love interest or losing the ability to fly? Make this big. I can't emphasize that enough. This should represent a significant change from the character's makeup in the beginning. The carefree farm girl who ran away without thinking how it would affect her aunt and uncle must now show that she cares enough to save her new friends. Dorothy has changed.

From this moment in the book your Hero is reborn. Like Orpheus he's descended into hell and made an ultimate sacrifice for something greater than himself. This can be a physical battle or a final showdown (in the case of a series not always) with the Shadow. Remember the Shadow can be external or internal. You can have more than one Shadow but the Shadow is not always the villain. The villain is sometimes an outward representation of the Shadow.

Your Hero cannot whine at this point. This is not a

Donkey Moment like the first Refusal. He had his chance way back at the beginning. He must do this willingly. His Allies may show up to help, but only after he's committed to his own death/defeat. Basically, the Hero thinks all is lost but he is going to give it his all anyway in the hopes that others can carry on. Even though he may die, Luke must commit to destroying the Death Star in order for the world as he knows it to survive. You can apply Spock's advice from Wrath of Khan. That is that logic clearly dictates that the needs of the many outweigh the needs of the few.

A good card here is the Star which illuminates the situation and brings revelation to the Hero. It shows that true salvation comes from above but also from within. Once the Hero has been resurrected, he knows that he has what he needs. It is an affirmation of his Journey. Another contender would be the Hanged Man with its theme of personal sacrifice. In fact, the Hanged Man can be seen as Christ on the cross which plays directly into the theme of resurrection.

Because the Star is the moment where you rise up and reach for your highest goals, I'm assigning it instead of the Hanged Man to this position. Your Hero has to reach higher and further than he thought possible. He must stretch for this because it is, in a very real sense, him being completely revamped.

This is often the step where your Hero is turned inside out. He must use everything he's learned on this journey. If he were a video game character, he'd be a level 12 or higher (grin). But truly, the Hero is transformed. Consider again the image of the Hanged Man. He's been turned upside down, literally. Everything looks different to him at this point. You do need to remember that this Resurrection must be believable. Your Hero must have struggled with this and grown throughout your story. Otherwise you will let your readers down. Think of the times you have felt you knew a character only to have them do something so out-of-character that you wanted to fling the book at a wall. Don't do this to your reader.

For this multi-layered stopping point, you need to think the big test. One great essay I read said this was the Hero's final exam. If you've ever done oral boards, you have a glimpse of the trauma and pressure on the Hero at this point. Many stories use a physical representation of birth here. Luke has to fly through a narrow tunnel before he can zoom up into the vastness of space. The imagery is subtle but when you apply the overlay of how a baby passes through the vaginal canal out into the world, you can see the emphasis.

Good storytelling engages our subconscious selves as well as our conscious selves. Vogler mentions the hero must be seen to be clearly fighting for his life. I would add that in this case "life" could be the thing he fears losing the most. Sometimes drawing breath is less important than saving the girl. This is a cathartic cleansing moment. Remember that making your reader cry is a good thing. They need this as much as your hero does by this point if you've done your job. Having your hero shed tears here is never a bad idea. Hysterical laughter might also fit the bill.

Catharsis is also about the transformation. If your Hero never cracked a smile, let him do it now. Show how he is different at this point. Emphasize the changes that have gone on. Show how his being broken has made him whole again. This is also how the Ordeal failure becomes the Resurrection win. What couldn't be accomplished in the Ordeal must be finished here.

THE RESURRECTION SPREAD

1. Hold the card that you drew for the Resurrection out.
2. Please note that you will be using the FULL deck except for the Resurrection card for this reading. This varies from the ones you have done to this point.
3. Shuffle the deck at least 3-5 times.
4. Cut the deck into three piles.
5. Restack them so that the last cut is on top.
6. Draw two cards.
7. Lay the first one face-down to the left of the Resurrection card.
8. Lay the second one face-down to the right of the Resurrection Card.

Card One
The Resurrection Card
Card Two

Card One (To the left) is what your Hero feels he has failed at doing. Let this be his self-loathing card if you will. It's why he feels he shouldn't be allowed to resurrect. Use your Fear card from earlier in this chapter as well. It can be used to explain why he feels this way.

Card Two (To the right) demonstrates how he will be transformed by this event. Who will he become after this change? How will he look/feel/act? Compare this to the card you pulled for the Ordinary World. How does this answer how he was feeling about his circumstances then?

STORY TEMPLATE:

My hero, (name), started out in a world represented by (card). Now he has been called to adventure by (the card). But he refuses because (what reason does the card suggest?) The worst thing that could happen if he goes is (something from the card). His Mentor (card) taught him (card lesson) which made him realize (why he had to Cross The Threshold). Now my hero is going to be tested by (Test card). His Allies are represented by (Allies card). His Enemies are represented by (Enemies card). My hero faced the (Inmost Cave card). He faced his Ordeal which was (Ordeal card). He got his reward which was (Reward card.) The Road Back was represented by (Road Back card.)

My hero must understand that all of this has led him to become (Resurrection card.)

EXAMPLE:

For Micah's Resurrection, the King of Swords turns up. Again, this is Micah's inner self. He is manifesting as a man of action who is engaged and involved with those around him. He's changed from 6 of Swords running from troubled times to seek peace to a man who cares for his family and Pack.

Now shuffle your deck (if you used this full deck

for the Fear card, remove the twelve (if you only pulled one for the Tests, Allies and Enemies, you will only have ten) Journey cards and put them into the arch.) You only have one stop left on your Hero's Journey after this. Once you've pulled this card and laid it into the arch, pull back a bit and look at it in conjunction with the other cards. What do you see? Anything in terms of the way figures are facing or a repetitive motif?

QUOTE

"It is good to have an end to journey toward; but it is the journey that matters, in the end."
-- ~Ernest Hemingway

JOURNAL PROMPT

What journeys have you taken that stick with you? What journeys do you dream of taking? You might find pictures that represent both the past and the present. Write your travel memoirs.

Write with joy, y'all. The journey has to mean something. You could also write a journal entry from one of your other character point's of view. Have them describe your main character. Imagine how that hero looks to someone else who isn't as invested in them as you might be.

Chapter Thirteen

Return With The Elixir

Twas Pirelli's Miracle Elixir, that's what did the trick Sir, true Sir true, Was it quick Sir, did it in a tick Sir, just like an Elixir ought to do.
  -- Stephen Sondheim's Sweeny Todd: The Demon
     Barber of Fleet Street

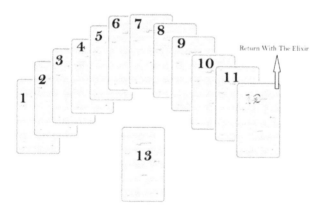

The Elixir, for me, has been one of the harder concepts. This is because it can be an intangible thing.

It's easier in a fantasy to identify this Elixir aka Reward. But in other genres of fiction, this item can be a bit murky. One way to define the Elixir is as something that will be useful to the Hero. More importantly, this knowledge will heal/help his community. His task now is to take this magic back. It's important to realize that it is not enough to get the Elixir. It must be returned.

Your Hero has been resurrected. He's a different person from the Hero who began this journey. Now he has to go back to that Ordinary World with the Elixir. This represents that final reward your Hero has earned. Note the word choice. Earned. Not given or received. Earned as in worked his rear off! As with the Resurrection, this is a big one. Your Hero deserves this moment of cheering crowds, long-wet-deep kisses, you call it--this is the Hero's moment in the sun.

Finally we have reached the moment of Happily Ever After (or in some cases Happy For Now.) Part of what happens here is that the Hero is conveying a greater awareness to the reader/audience of themselves. When Luke stands in front of everyone receiving a medal and accolades, we as the audience feel a sense of accomplishment. That is Luke's Return With The Elixir.

Let's think about this. Your Hero has been through hell and back. So has your reader if you've done your job as the storyteller. Now he must re-enter his Ordinary World. Some say he's been resurrected and purified. I say he's been shattered, reformed and is ready to continue forward. If you are writing a series, there may still be a crack in his sword or a shadow lurking in the wings. Never forget that your Hero has changed from the Hero who first got that Call to

Adventure. His community may not want him back, but he must return for this story to be complete.

In the Tarot, the card I would pull for this would be the Sun for the sense of celebration it conveys. The Sun traditionally features a baby on a white horse in direct opposition to the skeletal figure on the white horse on the Death card. There is an inherent idea of good health, joyful family--pretty much lots of good things coming the Hero's way. And as a reminder, if the Sun isn't handled carefully, the Hero could get burned. With the emphasis of this card on health and community, it is a natural for the Return with the Elixir stage.

I've seen this return referred to as "establishing the new order" which would also associate with the Sun because of the illumination part. When the Sun is that bright, the Shadow forces have to retreat. Remember that this is what your Hero has been tasked to bring back. This adds something to his Ordinary World. In a romance, a romantic partner would be this Elixir that changes him and his Ordinary World. In a mystery, it would be the solution which might include the punishment of the villain.

Comedies that are following the Hero's Journey may end with the Hero not learning and his last event is a repeat of what got him into trouble in the first place. Sometimes the boon is treasure won on the quest, or love, or just the knowledge that the special world exists and can be survived. Sometimes it's just coming home with a good story to tell.

Here is where you will wrap up any loose ends. Anything not revealed at this point should be revealed unless it is part of a larger series arc. Remember that the Hero's Journey will also occur over the series so it is always a good idea to map that out for yourself if you are doing a series. I would always make sure you have a Hero's Journey in each story, but backing up to look at the larger picture will be helpful.

One way of seeing how this Elixir changes your Hero is to consider what he's been through. His brushes with death should have given him an immediate need to live. He has faced death down so that fear should be lessened here. He sees the value of living and is willing to go for it now. Any wounds to his psyche from his life in his Ordinary World will be assuaged by this Elixir. Of course, he may be presented with new problems now. Think about the dull heroine no one ever looked at twice. Now she has blossomed. She goes from famine to feast which can create the next book in your series if you are not writing a stand-alone.

The Elixir is also for the villain in that it is exactly what the villain deserves. Make their punishment fit their crime exactly. A nice plot device is to have them hoisted on their own petard somehow. If they are a self-aggrandizing villain, let them have to work among the masses as one of the "little people." Do remember not to drag this out though. Your reader deserves their Elixir just as much as your Hero deserves it.

Things to think about with this part are how will the Ordinary World change with this Elixir? Have you tied up all your loose ends or left enough clues to make your reader want to read on? Have you left your reader feeling the way you want them to feel? That's in your hands. You as the storyteller get to manipulate the reader's feelings. Do not yank the rug out from under the reader. Now is not the time for someone to wake up and realize the entire book was a dream.

MAPPING THE HERO'S JOURNEY

What treasure has your Hero brought back? What is his Happily Ever After? How does it answer the original Call to Adventure?

Shuffle the cards. Cut the deck. Pull a card. As you lay this card at the end of your arc, pay attention to any small symbols that may connect back to the rest of this spread. You are looking for images that mean something to you and to the story. If this card reminds you of another card in your spread, consider that was the point where the identity of the Elixir was revealed. That may have been the romantic Hero's first inclination that they were more involved with their partner than they thought.

If you have not been doing the Story Template all along, take time now to go back and write one sentence for each card as it relates to the position. This will give you a very bare bones outline. Remember that it is the storyteller's duty to flesh those bones out. You want to engross your reader as you twist and torture your characters.

You can also draw cards for between the stages. Think of these as bridges or doors. You are looking ahead to see how you get from one to the next. And remember, that this is your true story end. You can epilogue if you like, but this is where the train stops. The emotional rollercoaster is done.

THE RETURN WITH THE ELIXIR SPREAD

1. Hold the card that you drew for Elixir out.
2. Please note that you will be leaving all of the cards for the main Hero's Journey out and shuffling the rest back in if you choose to do these spreads.

3. Shuffle the deck at least 3-5 times.
4. Cut the deck into three piles.
5. Restack them so that the last cut is on top.
6. Draw two cards.
7. Lay the first one facedown to the left of the Elixir card.
8. Lay the second one facedown to the right of the Elixir Card.

Card One
The Return With The Elixir Card
Card Two

Card One (To the left) is the Hero's moment in the Sun. What does that look like? Is it a kiss? A medal? A new car? A family? Is it what he wanted? How will he get it back?

Card Two (To the right) shows the down side. What new problems will arise for your Hero now that he's brought the Elixir back? If this is a stand-alone, use this for what happens to the Villain. In cases where the Villain is an internal part of the Hero, this may show how he adapts to this part of himself.

STORY TEMPLATE:

My hero, (name), started out in a world represented by (card). Now he has been called to adventure by (the card). But he refuses because (what reason does the card suggest?) The worst thing that could happen if he goes is (something from the card). His Mentor (card) taught him (card lesson) which made him realize (why he had to Cross The Threshold). Now my hero is going to be tested by (Test card). His Allies are represented by (Allies card). His Enemies are represented by (Enemies card). My hero faced the (Inmost Cave card). He faced his Ordeal which was (Ordeal card). He got his reward which was (Reward card.) The Road Back was represented by (Road Back card.) My hero realized that all of this has led him to become (Resurrection card.)

Finally, my hero can have (Elixir card.)

EXAMPLE:

Micah's return is Justice. This is the verdict that he is not a lone wolf. He wins both the woman and his goddaughter. Justice is served literally. Now he gets to move forward into his new life.

QUOTE

If you have other things in your life -- family, friends, good productive day work -- these can interact with your writing and the sum will be all the richer.
-- by David Brin

JOURNAL PROMPT

Who makes your world brighter, bigger, better?

Write with joy, y'all. Writers can't live in a vacuum. Make sure you take time out to be with your family and friends. Read good books. Enrich your life to enrich your writing.

Chapter Fourteen
Encore

Theme

Even on the drum level, it's all about stating your theme, going back to certain things that need to be emphasized, not doing fills for the sake of doing fills.
-- John Otto

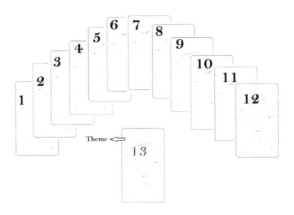

As our musical friend notes, theme is emphasizing what needs to be emphasized. It is the rhythm that you hear in a song from beginning to end even though the words may change. It's something that repeats throughout your story. In the movies I've used as examples, there are themes of anger and hate and how they change someone (Star Wars), self versus others (Shrek), believing in yourself (Wizard of Oz) and man versus nature (Avatar). While it can be argued that all of these movies include other important themes, these are ones that are easily identified.

In Wizard of Oz, none of the five main characters believe in themselves. "If I only had a..." is a recurring statement. Even the witch herself thinks she only needs the ruby slippers to have what she wants. As it turns out, all of them (except the witch for the bad must fail for the good to truly win) have what they needed within themselves. Shrek has to put aside his need to be alone to resolve the problem of the first movie. He cannot win the elixir if he doesn't save Fiona. Saving Fiona means he can't be alone. It's a classic dichotomy where the Hero has to change on a core level in order to become something more than he was at the start of his ordinary world.

This is a step I added to the Hero's Journey spread after working with several authors for their own stories as well as my own. I kept wanting some hint on how to tie things together. How to emphasize the journey's basic lesson for my Hero was something that was missing.

The question for me was how does our Hero's Journey reflect the theme of the novel. As writers, we hear about theme a lot. Sometimes we have a pat answer. The theme of Changing Hearts (11/7/2008) is redemption. But we actually didn't know that when we started writing. Cai and I tend to write the skeleton with some flesh and then go back through the story. We are looking for GMC for both major characters and the villain if there is one. Once we know the Goal, the Motivation and the Conflict, then we can start back into the manuscript and add more flesh until we have a fully conceived story.

Theme is one of those things that gets batted around a lot. You can just about bet on a workshop on "Finding The Theme" or some variation at any conference with the tag "writer". What is a theme?

In Writer's Inc, A Student Handbook For Writing And Learning, we are offered this not-so-clarifying definition:

"Theme is the statement about life a particular work is trying to get across to the reader. In stories written for children, the theme is often spelled out clearly at the end. In more complex literature, the theme will not be so clearly spelled out."

I don't know about you, but that doesn't really help me. A statement about life? Come on. I need something more concrete than that! Another definition volunteered that it is a recurring idea, a motif. This worked better for me because my mother was an interior designer. I understand motif far too well. It's that stamp that occurs throughout the story (house) that ties the whole house (story) together. The dragonfly doorknocker is echoed in the dragonfly dangling in the window and the one on the couch pillow and the one tucked into a nook in the bathroom and so on. NOTE: That was not my mother's idea of design. I just happen to love dragonflies.

A repeated thought or idea throughout your book can be a theme. What do you think another "Wizard of Oz" theme is? One might be self-sufficiency since all the major characters feel inadequate somehow. "Star Wars", for me, is also a theme of finding one's place. Take a moment to think of three movies you love. What are the themes? Remember these are big ticket items that affect the whole story. Many of the characters will echo the theme in their own journeys. This is something to remember actually. All characters have some type of journey to make even if the changes are subtle.

I can state that for me a theme is a recurring idea that is echoed throughout a story. This broad idea can be very blatant or, more often, quite subtle making you search for it. I think the best literary works are those that don't bash me over the head with the theme. I really like to put a book down or walk away from a movie that makes me think. The theme will come to me eventually as the one thing that was a take-away.

For instance, in "Stranger Than Fiction" I came away with the idea that we must live our lives without worrying about what others think or say. The main character kept hearing a running narration of his life. He had to decide if he was in control or if the voice was. So it could be said that the real theme is that of free will.

You can also say that themes arise from how the plot, setting, character, conflict, and tone entwine with one another. If you will allow me a moment of whimsy, the theme is the music that all the characters dance to. It is always there somehow in a good story. And I don't think that theme must be some deep, ominous, ponderous thing. It can be as light and silly as the theme of "The Importance of Being Earnest." And do consider Miss Prism's definition of fiction. She sums up the theme of that story quite handily. Yet another job you can hand off to a secondary character.

"The good end happily and the bad end unhappily. That is what fiction means."
-- Miss Prism, The Importance Of Being Earnest, Oscar Wilde

Of course, the same story may reflect different themes depending on the author. Matteo Bandello wanted his readers to know what dishonesty and disobedience could bring while one William Shakespeare had a very different message to convey in his retelling of Bandello's "Romeo and Juliet." Instead of teens who needed a serious time out for not honoring their families, Shakespeare re-imagined it as an epic tale of individuals vs. society. His take on this is that love is a good reason to disobey one's family.

Some popular literary themes are:
  Ambition
  Jealousy
  Beauty
  Loneliness
  Betrayal
  Love
  Courage
  Loyalty
  Duty
  Perseverance
  Fear
  Prejudice
  Freedom
  Suffering
  Happiness
  Truth

If we are talking about a motif or a theme, let's call this card the quintessence of the abstract. The pure, highly concentrated essence of a thing is what we are looking for here. Or, if you prefer a less highfalutin' way of saying this, then this card shows the overall point of the story.

In rereading this lesson, it has occurred to me that we may also get at the quintessence in a different way. Mary K Greer discusses the quintessence of a spread in her book *Tarot For Yourself.* This book is one of the most significant Tarot books of my life. I highly recommend it to anyone who would like to move further into the Tarot. In her book, she has this method of finding the quintessence card.

If you would like to try this method for finding your theme, do the following steps:

1. Lay out your arch of the Hero's Journey.
2. Write down the numbers for each card.
    1 for the Ace while the court cards remain numberless. The Fool is also numberless but each Major Arcana has a number associated with it.

If you have a deck where the Majors are not numbered, refer to the following list.

Major Arcana
    0 The Fool - choices offered
    1 The Magician - creative energy
    2 The High Priestess - mystery, hidden influences
    3 The Empress - abundance, fertility
    4 The Emperor - leadership, control
    5 The Hierophant - convention, society

6 The Lovers - love, relationships
7 The Chariot - mind over matter
8 Strength - courage, strength, power
9 The Hermit - wisdom, spirituality, inner seeking
10 Wheel of Fortune - unpredictability, changes
11 Justice - legal issues, balance
12 Hanged Man - withdrawal, rest
13 Death - change
14 Temperance - moderation, adaptation
15 The Devil - temptation, the material world
16 The Tower - conflict, problems
17 The Star - hope, inspiration
18 The Moon - unseen troubles
19 The Sun - marriage, success
20 Judgment - awakening, renewal
21 The World - success

3. Then add up your cards. If you get a number higher than 22, add those numbers together. For instance, 102 would be 1+0+2=3 and 39 would be 3+9=11. That final number of 22 or less is your quintessence or theme card for your novel. It will be one of the Major Arcana cards where 1 equals the Fool and 22 equals the World card.

If you do that method, do not do the following method.

Shuffle your cards. Focus on your story. Cut the cards into three piles then draw the first card and dive in. A good exercise now is to break your story down into one sentence for each card. Here's an example. Jack has never had to work a day in his life because he is the beloved youngest son of a millionaire (Fool). His heart is broken by a woman who leaves him because he has no responsibility (3 of Swords). He tries to forget her by opening up his own business (Ace of Pentacles). He hires a strange old man who tells him he is the son of a Fairy Queen and was kidnapped at birth (King of Cups). And so on.

Chapter Fifteen

Journals

Now that you have established a pattern of how to learn the Tarot and build your knowledge along with your trust of your own intuition, let's talk about Tarot journals. Tarot journals, for me, are something every student should keep. And I think we are all students. My current Tarot journal is full of spreads and thoughts on readings. As you start your Tarot journal, know that you join the many of us who also utilize this unique tool for opening up the world of Tarot for ourselves. I use mine as a learning aid as well as a meditation tool. Not to mention a place to jot down story idea and character thoughts.

But this first journal will be a study aid. You will need the basics. Something to write with and something to write on not to mention a Tarot deck-- these will be your three basic necessities. You may want to use an old deck (check flea markets, used bookstores, Craigslist, etc.) or you can buy a duplicate of the one you are studying with. For my study journal, I used a large 8.5 x 11 blank art book for this project. The very front page is your title page. Take a deep breath. This is your Fool's leap (and I promise it will all be good.)

Find the courage to write on the first page. That is the hardest thing for many of us -- "ruining" that lovely white paper with ink. But it has to be done! I offer you this exercise to begin.

On the very first page of your journal write your name. Now place an apostrophe and then the letter 's'. Now write Tarot Journal.

WHOA! Get out of town. Just like that, you have just named your journal. Mine reads Arwen's Tarot Journal. It may seem silly, but you have to break that barrier first! Do use stamps and colored pens/ pencils etc. if you feel like decorating. Remember that no one will be looking at this journal unless you allow them.

On the next page, write Table of Contents. Enter "The Journal Spread" on the first line. That's the first thing in your Tarot Journal. Now skip three to five more pages. That's where you will list your contents. Do the following spread. Write it down on the page.

The Journal Spread

1. What Will I Learn From This Journal?
2. What Will Block Me From This Journal?
3. Why Is This Journal Important?

The cards are laid out in order in a row. Write the spread name and the questions along with what cards show up in those positions. Use the techniques you've learned in this workbook if you get a card you aren't familiar with. Let your mind go and write. As before, no one is judging you.

Now remember that spare or old deck? After you finish your journal spread, label the next page 0 The Fool. If you have the deck, glue the Fool on this page.

Random Tip: I put four cards in the upper left corner then moved to the upper right corner for the next four page. Then four cards on the bottom left pages and four followed that on the bottom right pages. Then I rotated through that sequence until all 78 cards were in the book. For me, I only allowed the front and back of each page for this first journal. You may want to allow more. Totally up to you.

You have started with the Major Arcana. Next are the suits. I suggest the following order: Swords, Wands, Cups, Coins.

And that's it. That's the bones of your first Tarot Journal. You don't need much else unless you are a crafty type. Remember your journal doesn't have to be a fancy handmade book. You can use a .99 cent notebook from the local Whatever-Mart. It's your journal, your journey, and no one else needs to see it.

Back to the pages with the cards. What to do with them?

Write in the journal. Use your Am/Pm Tarot work to jot down important ideas. Create poems for each card. Oh yeah, you're marking up pages. You might even have to scratch a word out. I give you permission to have ink blotches and misspellings and stick figures that don't even look like sticks. I give you permission to draw when you don't want to write and to write when you don't want to draw. You can glue collages here. You can use gel pens in flaming pink or blackest black. You can use a super fine point or a thick magic marker. The key is to USE something so you are working on your journal.

Random Tip: Use the same color for the titles of the twenty-two Major Arcana and a color for each suit. This will help you when you are flipping through looking for things. Or color the upper right corner as a marker for each group.

Interpret them. Jot your interpretations down in the journal. And note, I said YOUR interpretations-- not the LWB's. The Little White Book has its place in the world, but this isn't one of them.

Don't worry about making long in-depth entries here. Just slap down on the paper what you get from the cards. Draw pictures in your journal of what the cards look like or what leaps out at you from the cards. Again, there is no wrong way of doing this unless you are just not doing it. Crayons or colored pencils might be fun to have on hand. What color is the strongest for you when you look at the card you drew?

All you are doing here at first is writing down what YOU see in the card. You can look at the LWB once you have finished that and add information from there so leave some room.

By the way? This may be something that is never complete. Let yourself be okay with that if you can. Tarot is an ongoing learning process for me. I started in 1981. You do the math.

Chapter Sixteen
Tarot Tools

Major Arcana

The Tarot is comprised of two parts. There are twenty-two cards that are not a part of any of the four suits. These are called the Major Arcana. To deepen your knowledge of Tarot and to use it for your writing, you may want to create a list of key words for the cards. Here are my own key words/phrases for the twenty-two Major Arcana.

If you want to delve into the Tarot more, you can do the following exercise for each Major Arcana (and the minor if you like). For this, I recommend a journal dedicated to Tarot studies.

Write down the name of the card. Then list two to four key words that make sense to you. That's important. This isn't about what may work for someone else. It is about what works for you. I advocate for coming up with at least two negative and two positive. Every card, to me, has some of the good and the bad.

Then list symbols that you see and what those symbols mean to you. Remember to focus on your interpretations rather than a catholic approach. This is where you determine if a dog means loyalty or danger depending on your personal experiences.

Finally, formulate two to three questions that this card evokes for you. You can also use the ones I have included for you below.

I have included the astrological correspondences as well as the place of the twenty-two Major Arcana on the Tree of Life. I am not Kabbalist so these are simply for your reference. There is some discussion within the Tarot community about some of these correspondences. You may come across other schools of thought.

0 Fool

Key Words:
> Imprudent, Hasty, Adventuresome, naive; carefree; adventurous
> Astrological Correspondence: Uranus
> Tree of Life Correspondence: Aleph path to Kether (Crown) & Chokmah (Wisdom)
> The Fool might represent an adventurer or a stunt person.

Some symbols to be aware of:
> The bag which means what I am willing to carry with me
> The dog which stands for who will take this journey with me

Key Questions:
> If the bag is full, what's in it?
> If the bag is empty, why is he carrying it?

If it is half-empty, are you an optimist or a pessimist?
What lesson do I seek to learn at this time?
What is holding me back from moving forward?
What possibilities lie ahead?

You do the work:
What do you think the sun or mountains or horizon mean? What are other symbols in this card? How would you interpret them? What is another job that the Fool might enjoy? Come up with one more question that you think you should be aware of when you see this card. You can use your own keywords as a basis for this.

I Magician

Key Words:
Power, Awareness, Application, Resourcefulness, Action
Astrological Correspondence: Mercury
Tree of Life Correspondence: Beth path to Kether (Crown) &
Binah(Understanding)
The Magician might represent a wizard or a physicist.

Some symbols to be aware of:
Infinity symbol: Energy is infinite. There is no end.
Ouroboros: Infinite possibilities.

Key Questions:
Am I using my power for the highest good?

What action do I need to take at this moment?
What am I missing in my day-to-day awareness?

You do the work:
What do you think the four symbols of the suits mean? What are other symbols in this card? How would you interpret them? What is another job that the Magician might enjoy? Come up with one more question that you think you should be aware of when you see this card. You can use your own keywords as a basis for this.

II High Priestess

Key Words:
Knowing, Psychic, Oracle, Secretive, Influential, Power-Hungry
Astrological Correspondence: Moon
Tree of Life Correspondence: Gimel path to Kether (Crown) & Tiphareth (Beauty)
The High Priestess might represent a spy or a private investigator.

Some symbols to be aware of:
Cross: Four directions, four elements, the place where the crossroads meet
Moon: female, secrets

Key Questions:
What does the Universe want me to know right now?
How can I learn to hear my own inner voice?
What secrets do I need to keep?
Who is keeping secrets from me and why?

You do the work:
What do you think the scroll and the columns mean? What are other symbols in this card? How would you interpret them? What is another job that the High Priestess might enjoy? Come up with one more question that you think you should be aware of when you see this card. You can use your own keywords as a basis for this.

WRITER TIP:

Some say that the Empress is the heart of femininity while the Priestess is the head. Something that occurred to me is that the High Priestess is the plotter variety writer while the Empress is the pantster.

III Empress

Key Words:
   Femininity, Abundance, Creativity, Nurture, Smothering, Overwhelming
   Astrological Correspondence: Venus
   Tree of Life Correspondence: Daleth path to Binah (Understanding)& Chokmah (Wisdom)
   The Empress might represent a surrogate mother or a kindergarten teacher.

Some symbols to be aware of:
   Shield: protected by love
   Wheat: that which feeds us

BONUS:

Compare the Empress' Cross w/ Heart to the High Priestess' Cross. What do you gather from that?

Key Questions:
   What does it meant to nurture and be nurtured?
   Who do I nurture? How do I nurture myself?
   How does abundance look in my life right now?

You do the work:
   What do you think of the water? What are other symbols in this card? How would you interpret them? What is another job that the Empress might enjoy? Come up with one more question that you think you should be aware of when you see this card. You can use your own keywords as a basis for this.

IV Emperor

Key Words:
   Strategy, Father, Authority, Practicality, Unyielding
   Astrological Correspondence: Aries
   Tree of Life Correspondence: Tzaddi path to Yesod (Foundation) & Netzach (Victory)
   The Emperor might represent a military higher up or a CEO.

Some symbols to be aware of:
   Beard: stature through age
   Ram: initiative, determination and taking action

Key Questions:
>   When you pull this card, consider the following questions:
>   What practical solutions am I missing?
>   How is my relationship with my father affecting this question?
>   Who do I need to protect or empower?

You do the work:
>   What do you think of his staff? What are some other symbols that are important to you in this card? What is another job that the Emperor would enjoy? Come up with one more question that you think you should be aware of when you see this card. You can use your own keywords as a basis for this.

V Hierophant

Key Words:
>   Respect, Knowledge, Hidebound Conformity, Ceremony
>   Astrological Correspondence: Taurus
>   Tree of Life Correspondence: Vav path to Chokmah (Wisdom) & Chesed (Mercy)
>   The Hierophant might represent a teacher or a CFO.

Some symbols to be aware of:
>   Hand: Blessing of love and spiritual well-being
>   Keys: Keys to the kingdom

Key Questions:
> Are my beliefs helping or hindering me?
> Am I disciplined and committed to spiritual development?
> Who do I look up to or who is my mentor in spiritual matters

You do the work:
> What do you think the staff or the people bowing before him mean? What are other symbols in this card? How would you interpret them? What is another job that the Hierophant might enjoy? Come up with one more question that you think you should be aware of when you see this card. You can use your own keywords as a basis for this.

VI Lovers

Key Words:
> Union, Trust, Temptation, Vulnerability, Spiritual Connection
> Astrological Correspondence: Gemini
> Tree of Life Correspondence: Zain path to Binah (Understanding) & Tiphareth (Beauty)
> The Lovers might represent a wedding planner or a prostitute.

Some symbols to be aware of:
> Angel: Spiritual needs
> Lily: Purity and innocence

Key Questions:
> Who do you truly trust?
> Who do you need to communicate with on a deeper level?
> Who needs your vulnerability right now?

You do the work:
> What do you think their nudity means? What are other symbols in this card? How would you interpret them? What is another job that the Lovers might enjoy? Come up with one more question that you think you should be aware of when you see this card. You can use your own keywords as a basis for this.

VII Chariot

Key Words:
> Action, Control, Focused, Driven, Hasty
> Astrological Correspondence: Cancer
> Tree of Life Correspondence: Cheth path to Binah (Understanding) & Geburah (Severity)
> The Chariot might represent an entrepreneur or a bus driver.

Some symbols to be aware of:
> Chariot: Speed and instinctive action
> Breastplate: Divine Guidance

Key Questions:
> Where am I out of control?
> Where am I in control?
> Where should I be headed?

You do the work:
What do you think the animals pulling the chariot mean? What are some other symbols that are important to you for this card? What is another job that the Chariot might enjoy? Come up with one more question that you think you should be aware of when you see this card. You can use your own keywords as a basis for this.

VIII Strength

Key Words:
Courage, Patience, Compassion, Domination, Defeating
Astrological Correspondence: Leo
Tree of Life Correspondence: Teth path to Geburah (Severity) & Chesed (Mercy)
Strength might represent a doctor or a bouncer.

Some symbols to be aware of:
Lion: Fundamental needs and wants
Lady: Taming the Beast

Key Questions:
How are you controlled by your physical needs?
Where are you fighting the most self-battles?
What area of your life are you strongest in?

You do the work:
What do you think of the mountains or the wreath? What are some other symbols that are important to you in this card? What is another job Strength might

enjoy? Come up with one more question that you think you should be aware of when you see this card. You can use your own keywords as a basis for this.

IX Hermit

Key Words:
> Key Words: Wisdom, Solitude, Withdrawn, Detachment, Searching
> Astrological Correspondence: Virgo
> Tree of Life Correspondence: Yod path between Tiphareth (Beauty) & Chesed (Mercy)
> The Hermit might represent a professor or a mad genius.

Some symbols to be aware of:
> Lantern: Light of learning
> Hood: Type of mental/spiritual cave

Key Questions:
> What do you need to seek more wisdom on?
> In what area of your life do you need to seek more stillness?
> Who is your guide? Whom do you guide?

You do the work:
> What do you think of the staff of the hermit? What are some other symbols that are important to you in this card? What is another job that the Hermit might enjoy? Come up with one more question that you think you should be aware of when you see this card. You can use your own keywords as a basis for this.

X Wheel of Fortune

Key Words:
> Luck, Chance, Change, Destiny, Revolution, Consequence
> Astrological Correspondence: Jupiter
> Tree of Life Correspondence: Kaph path to Cheed (Mercy) & Netzach (Victory)
> The Wheel of Fortune might represent a psychic or a salesman.

Some symbols to be aware of:
> Sphinx: Wisdom and Riddles
> Wheel: Things change

Key Questions:
> How can you turn the wheel of fortune in your favor?
> What riddles do you need to solve before moving forward?
> What are the consequences of your current line of action?

You do the work:
> What do you think the four corner figures represent? What are other symbols in this card? How would you interpret them? What is another job the Wheel of Fortune might enjoy? Come up with one more question that you think you should be aware of when you see this card. You can use your own keywords as a basis for this.

XI Justice

Key Words:
   Truth, Fairness, Equality, Accountability, Unyielding
   Astrological Correspondence: Libra
   Tree of Life Correspondence: Lamed path to Geburah (Severity) & Tiphareth (Beauty)
   Justice might represent a lawyer or a judge.

Some symbols to be aware of:
   Crown: Legal authority.
   Scale: Balance and measurement

Key Questions:
   What do I need to examine more closely in my life?
   How am I not being fair to myself?
   Am I being honest with myself?

You do the work:
   What do you think the sword means? What are other symbols in this card? How would you interpret them? What is another job that Justice might enjoy? Come up with one more question that you think you should be aware of when you see this card. You can use your own keywords as a basis for this.

XII Hanged Man

Key Words:

   Yield, Surrender, Sacrifice, Non-Action, In-Between, Delay

Astrological Correspondence: Neptune
Tree of Life Correspondence: Mem path to Geburah (Severity) & Hod (Splendor)
The Hanged Man might represent an office worker or a researcher.

Some symbols to be aware of:
Halo: Represents enlightenment. "Fire in the head"
Upside Down: symbolizes changing your view.

Key Questions:
What do you need to sacrifice?
How can you change your view?
What do you need to yield to?

You do the work:
What do you think the crossed legs indicate? What are some other symbols that are important to you in this card? What is another job that the Hanged Man might enjoy? Come up with one more question that you think you should be aware of when you see this card. You can use your own keywords as a basis for this.

XIII Death

Key Words:
Change, Transition, Termination, Inevitability
Astrological Correspondence: Scorpio
Tree of Life Correspondence: Nun path to Tiphareth (Beauty) & Netzach (Victory)
Death might represent an assassin or a divorce lawyer.

Some symbols to be aware of:
    Skull: Emptiness
    Bishop: Ultimate authority of man before God

Key Questions:
    What do I need to change that is going to hurt?
    What do I need to terminate in my life?
    What is inevitable in this situation?

You do the work:
    What do you think the rose or child mean? What are some other symbols that are important to you in this card? What is another job that Death might enjoy? Come up with one more question that you think you should be aware of when you see this card. You can use your own keywords as a basis for this.

IXV Temperance

Key Words:
    Balance, Overdoing, Moderation, Blending
    Astrological Correspondence: Sagittarius
    Tree of Life Correspondence: Samech path to Tiphareth (Beauty) & Yesod (Foundation)
    Temperance might represent a bartender or a mediator.

Some symbols to be aware of:
    Cups: Alchemist at work
    Feet: Between worlds

Key Questions:
>   Where am I out of balance?
>   How can I create more harmony and balance in my world?
>   Where can I draw more energy from?

You do the work:
>   What do you think the wings signify? What are some other symbols that are important to you in this card? What is another job Temperance might enjoy? Come up with one more question that you think you should be aware of when you see this card. You can use your own keywords as a basis for this.

XV Devil
>   Key Words: Ego, Bondage, Addiction, Illusion, Escape
>   Astrological Correspondence: Capricorn
>   Tree of Life Correspondence: Ayin path to Tiphareth (Beauty) & Hod (Splendor)
>   The Devil might be a drug pusher or a Dominant.

Some symbols to be aware of:
>   Inverted Pentagram: Sign of body over mind
>   Chains: Enslavement to base needs

Key Questions:
>   What enslaves me?
>   Where can I free of my addictions?
>   Who holds my chains?

You do the work:
> What do you think the way the Devil holds his hand means? What are other symbols in this card? How would you interpret them? What is another job that the Devil might enjoy? Come up with one more question that you think you should be aware of when you see this card. You can use your own keywords as a basis for this.

XVI Tower

Key Words:
> Inspiration, Upheaval, Cataclysm, Sudden Shift
> Astrological Correspondence: Mars
> Tree of Life Correspondence: Peh path to Hod (Splendor) & Netzach (Victory)
> The Tower might represent a rebel or a corporate takeover specialist.

Some symbols to be aware of:
> Lightning: Unexpected
> Fire: Being consumed

Key Questions:
> What warning signs am I ignoring?
> What am I building up that isn't steady?
> How can I minimize upcoming explosions?

You do the work:
> What do the falling figures mean to you? What are other symbols in this card? How would you interpret them? What is another job that the

Tower might enjoy? Come up with one more question that you think you should be aware of when you see this card. You can use your own keywords as a basis for this.

XVII Star

Key Words:
> Hope, Promise, Overreaching, Rising, Overpromising
> Astrological Correspondence: Aquarius
> Tree of Life Correspondence: Heh path to Tiphareth (Beauty) & Chokmah (Wisdom)
> The Star might represent an actor or a trust fund baby.

Some symbols to be aware of:
> Bird: Messages
> Water: Replenishment

Key Questions:
> How can I find hope in this situation?
> How can I best rise above all of this?
> What do I need to reach for?

You do the work:
> What do you think the position of the figure means? What are other symbols in this card? How would you interpret them? What is another job that the Star might enjoy? Come up with one more question that you think you should be aware of when you see this card. You can use your own keywords as a basis for this.

XVIII Moon

Key Words:
Cycles, Emotion, Reflection, Confusion, Illusion
Astrological Correspondence: Pisces
Tree of Life Correspondence: Qoh path to Netzach (Victory) & Malkuth (Kingdom)
The Moon might represent a spy or a psychologist.

Some symbols to be aware of:
Dog: Tame
Wolf: Wild

Key Questions:
How are my emotions affecting this issue?
What part of myself am I neglecting?
What do I need to look at more clearly?

You do the work:
What do you think the shellfish represents? What are other symbols in this card? How would you interpret them? What is another job that the Moon might enjoy? Come up with one more question that you think you should be aware of when you see this card. You can use your own keywords as a basis for this.

XIX Sun

Key Words:
Life, Energy, Growth, Clarity, Vibrancy, Understanding, Illumination, New Beginnings, Breaking Through

Astrological Correspondence: Sun
Tree of Life Correspondence: Resh path to Hod (Splendor) & Yesod (Foundation)
The Sun might represent a politician or a family counselor.

Some symbols to be aware of:
Sunflower: Follow Life
Baby: Beginnings

Key Questions:
How can I grow more?
What dark corners do I need to shine more light into?
What is the most important thing I am beginning?

You do the work:
What do you think the crown on the baby's head means? What are other symbols in this card? How would you interpret them? What is another job that the Sun might enjoy? Come up with one more question that you think you should be aware of when you see this card. You can use your own keywords as a basis for this.

XX Judgment

Key Words:
Judgment, Resurrection, Transformation, Karma
Astrological Correspondence: Pluto
Tree of Life Correspondence: Shin path to Hod (Splendor) & Malkuth (Kingdom)
Judgment might represent an undertaker or a contest judge.

Some symbols to be aware of:
Arms: Ascending
Sky: Another plane of existence

Key Questions:
What call do I need to listen to?
Who am I judging?
Why am I being judged?

You do the work:
What do you think the open graves represent? What are other symbols in this card? How would you interpret them? What is another job that Judgment might enjoy? Come up with one more question that you think you should be aware of when you see this card. You can use your own keywords as a basis for this.

XXI World

Key Words:

Success, Overdoing, Enrichment, Lacking Spirituality
Astrological Correspondence: Saturn
Tree of Life Correspondence: Tau path to Yesod (foundation) & Malkuth (Kingdom)
The World might represent a traveler or a philanthropist.

Some symbols to be aware of:
Corner Figures: Archangels
Oval: Circle of life

Key Questions:
   How can I best enrich my world?
   What do my friends bring to me that I am not aware of?

You do the work:
   What else could the four corner figures represent? What are other symbols in this card? How would you interpret them? What is another job that the World might enjoy? Come up with one more question that you think you should be aware of when you see this card. You can use your own keywords as a basis for this.

Here is a spread to use for the hero or villain of your story. For this spread, use only the Major Arcana. Apply a keyword for each card in relation to the question.

TIP:

If you don't want to bother with pulling out your Majors, just shuffle and cut the deck. Pull until you get to a Major for each spot. Just ignore the minors along the way.

Fill-In-The-Blank Majors Spread

My hero wanted to be a (draw a card and use that card's job), but he had to change his mind because he had to learn (draw a card and use one of that card's questions). So instead he decided to become a (draw a card and use that card's job). When that didn't work out, he finally found (draw a card and use that card's job) which made him feel (draw a card and use one of that card's keywords).

EXAMPLE: Fill-In-The-Blank Majors Spread

My hero wanted to be a [JUDGMENT] judge, but he had to change his mind because he had to learn [SUN] What dark corners he needed to shine more light into. So instead he decided to become a [HIEROPHANT] teacher. When that didn't work out, he finally found he was better at being a [HERMIT] scientist which made him feel [TOWER] sudden shifts were the way to inspiration.

Chapter Seventeen

Minor Arcana

There are seventy-eight cards in a Tarot deck. Twenty-two are the Major, but the other fifty six comprise the Minor Arcana. There are many books out that enumerate each card with lengthy descriptions. What I offer here is a down-and-dirty interpretation of each card. This is not meant to be an exhaustive or in-depth discussion of the many layers of the cards. Each one could be a chapter by itself. This is simply for you to use when you get stuck when you are mapping out your Hero's Journey. Think of this chapter as your travel agent helping you out with some suggestions.

I will go through all fifty six cards including the court cards. One thing to note is that numerology plays a key role in how I personally read the Tarot. I do recommend getting a good book on numerology as well as astrology if you want to do more than read for your characters. Cards can be read upright or reversed. I don't read reversals in my professional consultations. I feel that there is enough to be read in the cards intuitively without turning them upside down. Other readers differ on this. I will give you the upright meaning followed by a few upright keywords. I will do the same for the reversals should you want to use them.

ACES

The Aces are the raw potential of the suit. I see them as the seed energy. These cards represent what energy could happen but may not have yet. The one of the suit, the Ace relates to the Magician in the Major Arcana.

Ace of Swords: "START"
Upright: New energy for new starts. Business, writing, intellectual pursuits, legal matters. Clarity of mind to matters at hand. The mind awakening for new challenges. Problem solving skills. New idea, New possibility, Intellectual opportunity, Creative thought.
Reversed: Not a good time to start a new project. Focus on editing, re-evaluating, checking all the fine details. Others could be opposed to this idea. Quarrels potentially. Foiled, Blocked, Quarrels, Irritation over minor details, Unfocused.

Ace of Wands: "BEGIN"
Upright: Ambition. Fertility (creating life, art, etc). A new spark of energy for a new passion. Optimistic answer. Intense energetic starts. Fresh passion. Birth, Spark, Creativity, Inventive
Reversed: Movement is blocked. Progression delayed. Possibly sexual misunderstandings. You want to change/develop but something is preventing that. Delays, Disappointments, Passion overruling logic

Ace of Cups: "OPEN"
Upright: New love, friendship. Emotional creativity. New happiness. Imagination is strong. Desire for a child or creation of child. New relationship, birth, love, beauty in creation

Reversed: One-sided interest. Emotionally draining. Loss of creative juice. Emotional co-dependency. Emotional loss, Chaos, Withdrawal, Imbalance, Emptiness

Ace of Pentacles: "GROW"
Upright: A new job or some type of new money potential. Financial improvement. Inheritance or unexpected windfall. New entrepreneur. Growth, Job, New/Found money, Loan approval.

Reversed: Hard times financially. Getting fired. Bad work environment. Greed, Hoarding, Scarcity, Declined

TWOS

The twos are the cards of balance or partnership. Generally there is a choice to be made or a change is called for. This is what happens when the seed energy attracts other energy. Growth happens and there are two. This card is related to the High Priestess who sits between the two pillars.

2 of Swords: "DEBATE"
Upright: Balanced but not resolved. An uneasy peace. A personal hard choice. Mental partnership but not physical. Clash of ideas or words. An internal battle of self. Venting, Tenuous peace, Hidden passions.

Reversed: Something not yet revealed. Impulsive actions not good. Information is hidden. Deceit, Impulsive, Lies

2 of Wands: "Spark"
Upright: Physical partnership without emotion. Passionate exchange. Energy high. Business Partnership, Negotiations, Contract, Work friendship, productive relationship
Reversed: External conflict, Difficult partnerships, they're just not that into you. Partnership Dissolution, Getting burned, False Victory

2 of Cups: "SHARE"
Upright: Recognition of love, of a friend or soul mate. Important new relationship. Balanced emotions that offer a place of connection. Love, Romance, Partnership, Friendship
Reversed: Emotional imbalance. Circular arguments. A time when no one understands anyone. Emotional battle, Dissolution, Needing a break.

2 of Pentacles: "BALANCE"
Upright: Business opportunity. The instinctive knowledge of how to juggle finances, a check book, or jobs. Second job. Second source of income. Financial "Angel". Financial balance, Entrepreneur, New Skills, Business developing.
Reversed: No work/personal balance. Hurry/Stop cycle. Financial fluctuations due to lack of budget and self-responsibility. Extra work, Lack of focus, Debts, Loss of income

THREES

Threes are groups and families. Relating to the Empress, this is the result of fertility (it takes two to create a third).

3 of Swords "HURT"
Upright: A relationship gone sour. Someone's been betrayed or has betrayed someone else. Traditionally the card of the broken hearted-lover. Heartache, Treachery, Backstabbing
Reversed: Things may not be as bad as you think. Leftover emotional pain. A reminder that you can and will heal from heartbreak. Healing, A new start, Emotional stress

3 of Wands: "WAIT"
Upright: Opportunities coming. Your ship is about to come in. Career or creative growth. Hard work rewarded. Success, Opportunity, Anticipation, Reward
Reversed: Standing around waiting for something to happen. Unrealistic wishes. Putting all your eggs in one basket. Delays, Unrealistic expectations, wanting a free ride

3 of Cups: "PLAY"
Upright: Life's happy celebrations. Joy. Parties with friends and family. Celebration, Family gatherings, Parties, Joy
Reversed: Too much fun. Too much partying. Overindulging. Unwise emotional commitments. Overindulging, Social Climbing, Irresponsible, Hungover

3 of Pentacles: "GROUP"

Upright: Group work. Presenting an idea to a committee. Rewarded for hard work and effort. Presentation, Committee approval, Recognition, Architect

Reversed: Working on the wrong project, Unwilling to invest time, No recognition for efforts. Denied. Lost bid.

FOURS

The Fours are squares which can be supportive or unyielding. They are related to the Emperor who is the number four card as well as the father figure.

4 of Swords "SOLITUDE"

Upright: A need for rest and recuperation. Shut down the mental noise. Meditation, Rest, Withdrawal, Healing, Mental quiet, Recuperation time, getting away from it all.

Reversed: Forced downtime such as being locked away in solitary confinement. Left with only your thoughts for company. Isolation, Imprisonment, Mental unease, Nervous exhaustion

4 of Wands "FOUNDATION"

Upright: Stability of a home. Four walls surrounding you. Success and security and a loving place to live. Strong foundations. Time to celebrate success in your life. Foundation, stability, Manifesting dreams, Successful birth.

Reversed: Delays on finding a home. Leaving too many loose ends. Taking a time out on chasing your dreams. Unrealistic pursuits, Poor planning, Taking the easy way out. Shoddy work.

4 of Cups "STAGANATION"
Upright: Regret and dwelling on what you have lost. Learning to let go of what you never had. Dissatisfaction, despair, Lack of emotional commitment. Disappointment. Emotionally drained. Relationships dissatisfaction. Ennui. Fear of risking hurt.
Reversed: You don't want to be alone. Need to fill the emptiness. Taking on emotional responsibilities that mean nothing. Needing an emotional shake-up. Fear of being alone, New hobby, transitory emotional attachments

4 of Coins "GREED"
Upright: Budgeting skills necessary. Be careful with money. Overly focused on material wealth. Budget, Monetary responsibility, modest returns, financial stability. Fear of losing
Reversed: Greed and overspending. Misplaced generosity. Strapped for cash. Worrying about bills so much that there is no joy anymore. Greed, Miser, Money woes

FIVES

Fives are what happens when you have stability (four) and add one more thing. Sometimes that's an upset but sometimes it's the energy that encourages growth.

5 of Swords "STRIFE"
Upright: Competitive situation. Learning to win

at all costs or to surrender wisely. Battle may be won, but the war is not over. Lies, gossip and negative thoughts. Power struggle, Strife, Collateral damage

Reversed: Time to cut your losses. You've already lost so walk away. Learning from defeat. Acceptance, Surrender, Walking Away, Disengaging

5 of Wands "STRUGGLE"

Upright: Competition for limited item. Athletic matches. Challenges from others. Animated discussions about things that matter. Family in flux mode. Arguments with a purpose. Debate, Conflict, Arguments, Competition

Reversed: Possible internal conflicts at work. Contracts being hammered out. Unnecessary power struggles. Internal conflict, Shadow negotiations, Cheating

5 of Cups "LOSS"

Upright: Obsessing over what is lost, rather than being glad for what remains. Crying over spilled milk. Being emotionally distant. Broken dreams, Emotional victimhood

Reversed: An emotional reunion or healing from the loss. Old friend of lover coming back. Taking a chance on being emotionally available. Emotional growth, Rebuilding, Healing, Opening up.

5 of Coins "EVICTION"

Upright: Financial ruin. Loss of health. Family on the street. Forced move. Denied sanctuary. Not asking for what you need. Poverty, Despair, Negative Balance

Reversed: Hard times can be overcome with hard work. Receiving help unasked for. Learning to love where you are. New faith, Financial aid, Reversing trends, Reaching out.

SIXES

The Sixes are balance and harmony. They are the energy of the three intensified.

6 of Swords "ESCAPE"
Upright: Leaving difficulties behind. Learning to accept help from others. Moving from turbulent times to calmer waters. Optimistic outlook for your future. Moving, Releasing. Escaping
Reversed: Trouble dogs your heels. Chaos is only avoided through dogged determination. If you have the tenacity to continue, you can get out of this trouble. Temporary solution but a breather at least. Struggle, Temporary peace, delayed travels.

6 of Wands "VICTORY"
Upright: Success in career. Good news arriving. Graduation. Long term work rewarded. Victory, Triumph, Winning
Reversed: Small failures will undermine your success. Victory snatched away. Keep on the path and don't stop. Unrewarded, Thwarted, Blocked.

6 of Cups "Nostalgia"
Upright: Childhood friends. Something/someone returning. Childhood, Emotional past,Ex-lovers, Old love
Reversed: Holding on to the past for the wrong reasons. Emotionally childish. Needing a fresh start. Stuck in the past, Fear of the future, Innocence lost.

6 of Coins "GENEROSITY"

Upright: Tangible gift. Offer of help. Give and take. Give and take creates balance and harmony. Generosity the generosity of giving and receiving. Generosity, Giving, Philanthropy, charity

Reversed: Gift with strings attached. Loss of expected money. Dying intestate. Gambling. Expecting the lottery.

SEVENS

The sevens are related to the Chariot. In that sense, they can reveal that you are in a situation where you need to exercise more control or that you can't control.

7 of Swords "THIEF"

Upright: Caution against sharing ideas. Mind going so fast you may miss things. Sneaky bastard taking something. Intellectual theft, Corporate raider, too much to think about.

Reversed: Make sure the product matches the pitch. Hyping something up. Con artist. Hard choices. Seek the real truth. Tricks, Schemes, Hype.

7 of Wands "DEFEND"

Upright: Take the high ground. Hold your position. Feeling like it's you against them. Tenacity, Right Road, David/Goliath.

Reversed: Not having faith in your ability to persevere. Allowing others to take over your world. Fear of failure, Insecurity, Puppet.

7 of Cups "DECIDE"

Upright: Can't make up your mind. Overwhelmed with emotional choices. Waiting is advised. Daydreams, Wait and see, Illusions

Reversed: You are allowing your fantasies to remove you from reality. Overindulging in addictive substances is also highlighted here. Not connected or grounded at all. Addictions, Out Of Touch, Seeing only what you want to see.

7 of Coins "GARDENING"

Upright: The pause between weeding and harvesting. Recognizing hard work accomplished. Weed what is unnecessary. Project that needs to be completed. Weed, Growth, Increase.

Reversed: Hard work not paying off. Being drained by work. Choked out by weeds. Ned to break to reassess. Unpaid work, No reward, Wrong direction, Being used.

EIGHTS

The Eights are associated with Strength. Here are cards associated with hard choices and hard work.

8 of Swords "PERILS"

Upright: Feeling trapped. Feeling as if you can't move. Mental blocks, Stuck, Not Seeing.

Reversed: A new way of thinking about an old problem. Moving in a different direction. Standing up for yourself. Being a survivor. Release, New start, Fresh ideas.

8 of Wands "JOURNEY"

Upright: Change of direction. Fast movement. Unexpected travel. Rapid change. Blocks removed. Blocks removed suddenly. Travel, Expanding horizons, Changes, Movement, Expansion.

Reversed: Detours and delays combined with miscommunication. A caution to slow down and think twice. Possible cancellations of travel plans. Delay, Strikes, Miscommunication, Energy drains.

8 of Cups "REGRET"

Upright: Letting go of old emotional baggage. Potentially separation or divorce. Time to walk away. Release, Grow up, Move on.

Reversed: Rejecting emotional help. Confusion about what is real and what is not. Shutting out others. Rejection, Depression, Confusion.

8 of Coins "STUDENT"

Upright: Learning something new. Learning/teaching as in the apprentice/journeyman/master levels. Starting over or second career track. Building on what you know. Apprenticeship, New skills, Education, Workmanship.

Reversed: Working hard without pleasure. You don't feel as if your work counts. You are feeling stagnant or stuck where you are. No opportunity for advancement. Limited at work, Dishonesty in business, bad training.

NINES

The Nines are related to the Hermit. These four

focus on reviewing what's been done. This can be something you have earned or been given.

9 of Swords "WORRY"
Upright: Being overwhelmed, nightmares, blowing things out of proportion. Completion worries, nightmares and anxieties. Your biggest task is to figure out which ones are real and which ones are manufactured. Then you have to face them down. Mental distress turning into physical illness. Nightmare, Stress, Worry, Tail chasing
Reversed: worries and stress fading finally. You have to practice mental housecleaning and get rid of unfounded fears. Harmony is coming back to your life. Facing fears, Abandoning worry, New solutions found

9 of Wands "CHALLENGE"
Upright: Will I ever get to the top? Stopping after hard work (you climb flight after flight of stairs to get to the top). Feeling like you may never finish the task at hand. Needing one last burst of energy to get to the final piece. Accepting success but preparing for the next task. Perseverance, Forging on, One last challenge
Reversed: the stress of a long struggle. You want to finish, but pressing ahead could cause physical illness. Mental exhaustion, Delays, Overworked.

9 of Cups "WISH"
Upright: Heart's desire. Your wish will come true. Decide what you really want. Emotional contentment--even bliss. Good things, good times and good people in your life. Enjoy. Joy, Harmony, Bliss
Reversed: Taking your current good times for

granted. Substance abuse. Risking everything. Smug, Overindulging, Ungrateful.

9 of Coins "SATISFACTION"

Upright: Solo successful career. Reflecting on all you have. Do something nice for yourself. Can be the little Empress. Success, Reward, Payouts

Reversed: Living beyond your means. Money may be drying up. Bad or risky investments failing. Bad investments. Foreclosure, Downsizing, Underpaid.

TENS

The tens are the final card of the cards known as the pip cards. These are related the Wheel of Fortune. When you see a ten, consider that the element is complete whether good of bad.

10 of Swords "PINNED DOWN"

Upright: Gossip is ruining your reputation. You have become a victim. Believing Yes, things are as bad as you fear. This card means betrayed confidences, destruction of self-esteem and/or trust. Being pinned down. Can be an indicator that it is time get free from whatever is pinning you down. Gossip is shredding your reputation. Negativity, Gossip, Mislaid trust.

Reversed: This card means you need took within for the cause of your destruction. Your own mind is your worst enemy. Deeply held beliefs need to be re-evaluated. Pessimism may be taking over. Watch for self-fulfilling prophecies. Defeating old patterns, Pessimism, Self-fulfilling prophecies.

10 of Wands "DELEGATE"

Upright: Trying to take on too much. Failure to share duties. Ambition overwhelming you. Overwhelmed, Overtasked, Burdened

Reversed: Managing responsibilities fairly well. Stressed but handling it. Multi-tasking-you're doing it right. Promotion, Multi-tasking, Capable.

10 of Cups "HAPPINESS"

Upright: The white-picket-fence-two-kids-a-house-and-a-spouse card. Think Happily-Ever-After. Your emotional journey has been successful (including a connection with yourself. Abundant Joy, Happily Ever After, Emotional Successes

Reversed: Review pie-in-the-sky ideals. Not seeing eye-to-eye with partner. Having to move from emotionally safe place. Feeling distant from loved ones (physically and emotionally). Emotionally distant, Emotionally detached, Disassociation.

10 of Coins "PROSPERITY

Upright: Enough money to be comfortable. Prosperous business. Well-to-do. Investments coming to term. Financial security. Comfortable in physical things. Investment, Family business/money, Material comfort.

Reversed: Family financial matters need review. Unexpected loss in terms of money and comfort. Investments fail. Family asking too much of you. Financial drains, Taxes, Unexpected money holes.

Chapter Eighteen

Court Cards

The Court cards represent one of the hardest areas to grasp. Do they represent actual people? Do they represent actions? When I read for my clients, I would answer yes and yes. For the purposes of this book, I will limit it to actual people. This is because as a tool for writing, it seems more useful to have sixteen character types for your toolbox.

There are many varieties of names for the Court system. We will use the most standard of these which is the Rider-Waite-Smith version. That is Pages, Knight, Queens and Kings. Pages are androgynous and can be either male or female. We will also use that system of androgyny for the Knights.

The very names give away a lot about the courts. Pages are the youngest. Traditionally, a page could be as young as seven or eight in medieval times. Knights were the brash teenagers who were charging into adult hood. Queens and Kings were mature individuals.

When I see these cards in readings, I hold to this personal rule. Pages are children to the Querent. Knights are younger by five years or so (mentally or physically) while Queens are their age and Kings are older. I also do not assign gender to the cards at any level when reading professionally. This is because I find it limiting when I know a man can have what is stereotypically considered feminine traits and the same for a woman.

Elementally, Pages are Air. Knights are Fire. Queens are Water. Kings are Earth. You can see this in terms of the seasons of maturity as well. The East (Air) represents youth. The South (Fire) represents sexual maturity. Water represents the fertile years. That leaves Earth as the older years where more is produced. I will show you how that works on each court card.

Let's take a closer look at these sixteen Tarot characters.

PAGES

Pages are the youngest of the court cards. A traditional take on this card is that they represent messages and messengers. They are represented by Air as their element.

Swords:
This is an intellectual young person. Hermoine Granger of Harry Potter fame is an excellent example. The Page of this suit is inquisitive and a good puzzle solver. This court card is the Air card in the element of Air so it is the truest to the energy of the Suit. You can see it as the "ruling" court card in Swords. And with that much air, you can expect one character trait to be that of easily distracted.

Wands:

Passion is the name of the game for this page. He acts first and thinks second--if at all. Sticking with the Harry Potter theme, here is Mr. Ron Weasley. That flaming red hair is also a physical characteristic of this suit. This is the Fire card in the element of Air. Consider what happens when you add air to fire and you can sense the easily roused temper of this character.

Cups:

The dreamer and emotionally driven Harry Potter is a perfect Page of Cups. This card represents someone who lets love lead him. He is given to more than one love (Cho and Ginny for instance) while he really doesn't understand love. This is the Water card in the element of Air. You have bubbles and a tendency to overflow.

Pentacles:

The sturdy student type--the Page of Pentacles focuses on learning but may seem a bit dull to some. He isn't a fast thinker nor does he react without taking time to check both ways. I would submit Neville Longbottom as the best representative from Harry Potter. This Earth card in the element of Air isn't easily moved since Earth is so solid.

YOU DO THE WORK:

Using a movie or book that you are familiar with, list characters that would fit each of these positions. Consider using characters from your own WIP if you like. Remember that a character grows. Harry Potter certainly isn't the dreamy Page of Cups by the final book nor is Neville the slow mover.

KNIGHTS

The Knights are the cards that represent movement and travel. This is the age where many of us moved the most--going off to college, getting married, getting a new job, joining the military. They are represented by Fire as the element.

Swords:
A job for this Air in Fire court card might be pilot. Air is the suit but the Knights are Fire so this is Air in motion. Intellectual pursuits will attract a Knight of Swords. He might be a corporate raider or an entrepreneur. You could also find this card to be a holy roller. From Avatar, Max Patel would be a good example of this knight as a scientist who could go to battle for his ideas. This is the Air Force recruit.

Wands:
This is the ruling Knight because he is the element of Fire in the position of Fire. Passion rules him and sometimes burns him up. Good jobs for this Knight would be anything from Greenpeace Warrior to spitfire lawyer. Staying within the movie Avatar, Norm Spellman is a good example because of his tendency to rush into things with passion and to get angry easily. He also got over his anger just as swiftly. This is the Army recruit.

Cups:
This knight is often portrayed as a sailor or perhaps a pirate. Other jobs would be a stripper or a doctor--both are emotions and passions combined.

With the element of Water in position of Fire, Trudy Chacon of Avatar is a perfect example of a Knight of Cups. Not afraid of a fight, she still wouldn't fight for something she didn't believe in. This is the Navy recruit.

Pentacles:
The slowest of the movers, this is the Knight who uses a horse or his feet to move him around. He is slow to burn since he is Earth in Fire, but when he does commit, he's all in. He won't join a fight without being convinced it's the only thing to do. Here is Jake Sully who is torn between the human interlopers and the Na'vi. This is the Marine recruit.

YOU DO THE WORK:
Using a movie or book that you are familiar with, list characters that would fit each of these positions. Consider using characters from your own WIP if you like.

QUEENS

The court card that represents the age of parenthood is the Queen which is the element of Water. This is a nurturing, compassionate card that expresses the energy of the suit in a more emotional way.

Swords:
This queen is quick of thought and sharp of tongue. She is a socialite who uses sarcasm as easily as she applies lipstick. Her emotions are ruled by her

thoughts so you will have to offer her a well-thought out plan if you want her on your side. This is the element of Air in suit of Water which can be turbulent. This is often a widow when Reversed. Consider Ouiser Boudreaux (Shirley MacLaine's character in Steel Magnolias) is a good Queen of Swords.

Wands:
This queen is passionate and emotional. She is always doing something and can be a bit scattered at times. Her energy is her key. Her emotions are ruled by her passions so she will tell it like it is or cry with you. This is the element of Fire in the suit of Water. Truvy Jones (Dolly Parton's character in Steel Magnolias) is the perfect Queen of Wands for me.

Cups:
This is the queen who is in her natural element. She is nurturing, caring, compassionate and more than a little psychic. Her emotions rule her if she's not careful, but a competent Queen of Cups is a charming woman. This is the ruling queen since the element of Water is in the suit of Water. M'Lynn Eatenton (the Sally Fields' character in Steel Magnolia) embodies these qualities for the Queen of Water.

Pentacles:
This is the queen who is good with money, people and most likely to be the community organizer. Her emotions are ruled by her love of her family. She is an excellent business woman who tends to do things that are community or family oriented. This is the element of Earth in the suit of Water. Clairee Belcher

(as played by Olympia Dukakis in Steel Magnolias) is the quintessential Queen of Earth.

YOU DO THE WORK:
Using a movie or book that you are familiar with, list characters that would fit each of these positions. Consider using characters from your own WIP if you like.

KINGS

The eldest of the court cards, the Kings are the final expression of the energy of this suit. They are what the Ace (the seed) energy was destined to be. They are mature individuals who have lived life and deserve respect for their wisdom.

Swords:
Here is the intellectual ruler who takes care of his family, home and business using logic and rational thinking. He is not moved by emotional approaches. He is the element of flexible Air in the inflexible suit of Earth. A good representative would be the Professor from Gilligan's Island.

Wands:
Our passionate ruler is the King of Wands who has learned to control his passions so they don't control him. He can be loud and aggressive when things don't go his way. With the element of Fire in the suit of Earth, I see the Skipper from Gilligan's Island as the King of Wands.

Cups:

This king is the lover and the romantic ruler who rules from the heart first rather than the head. Logic doesn't count as much as what feels right. Emotional appeals will win the day with this King who is Water in suit of Earth. Mrs. Howell from Gilligan's is a perfect King of Cups because she has the authority of age and money but is easily swayed by emotions.

Pentacles:

The last king is often the banker or successful business man who also balances family matters. He is concerned with physical appearances and keeping up with the latest status symbols. As the natural ruler of the element of Earth in suit of Earth, I see Thurston Howell, III from Gilligan's Island as a very good King of Pentacles.

YOU DO THE WORK:

Using a movie or book that you are familiar with, list characters that would fit each of these positions. Consider using characters from your own WIP if you like.

ASSIGNMENT ONE:

What are two Upright/positive court cards that you see in yourself? Now find two negatives that you see in yourself.

ASSIGNMENT TWO:

Think of examples of real people for each court card. These can be famous people or people in your family and friends and work circle.

Chapter Nineteen

The Suits

Look at the suits/elements to know what world you are dealing with: work, money, practical stuff, or something emotional or mental?
-- Mary K. Greer

The second half of the Tarot is called the Minor Arcana. A direct correlation to the playing cards of today can be seen in these 56 cards. With four suits using an ace through king system, you can actually play Gin Rummy. Or as Steven Wright is often quoted as saying, "Last night I stayed up late playing poker with Tarot cards. I got a full house and four people died."

This handout will serve as an overview and introduction to the suits. I will list some common correspondences for each suit as well as some keywords. You will find some exercises that you can do for each suit.

SWORDS
    Season: Spring
    Direction: East
    Zodiac: Gemini, Libra, Aquarius

Element: Air
Realm: Mind
Tarot: Swords, Blades, Knives
Playing Card: Spades
Gender: Masculine

There is some discussion on what suit starts the Tarot. For me, I start with the suit that I associate with Spring or Air. Blades, Daggers, Knives or Spades -- those are just a few of the names of the minor arcana suit most often associated with the element Air. I associate Air with East and Spring. You may find alternatives to this but this is what works best for me. What follows will be a starting point. You will want to leave room in your journal for additional notes and thoughts as you deepen your study of the Tarot.

The suit of Air can be thought of as communication, intellect, rational thinking. It can also be seen as truth-seeking. Positive aspects would be courage, knowledge-seeking, and authority while the negatives might be aggression, nitpicking, over analytical and overbearing. Think of the Air suit as representing the intangibles of the mind. Air. It is probably the most difficult element to contain, control, and quantify.

If you get a large number of swords in a reading, then this might mean someone has many issues that they need to resolve mentally. I often see this in individuals who are in their heads a lot. Also, consider the saying that truth is a double-edged sword. We don't always like what we learn from an Air card. Other negatives could be a need for surgery or someone who is arrogant and aloof. What we think can be beautiful, uplifting thoughts or angry, ugly ones.

Using this for your characters and stories, you can use this suit in a very literal manner if you like. Consider all the functions of your mind--puzzle-solving, decision-making, analyzing, and inquiring. This is about legal things as well like contracts, legal proceedings and the court system as well as politics. You can also see the camaraderie of soldiers or the unhealthy dependencies of victims. Swords can suggest a need to cut to the heart of a matter and to think things through rationally, without emotion.

For your character readings, consider that Swords can challenge or warn. Protect or attack. This suit can indicate a need for Spiritual examination. When they show as warnings, you need to ask, "What could happen if change or spiritual insight is not heeded?" Also pay attention to any current life challenges as well as obstacles for the character. This suit cuts through to the truth with very little cushioning of the blow. It can demand new awareness and new perceptions.

Don't fall into the trap of automatically assigning "bad" to Air cards because of the violent association we have with swords. Again, this is an element of communication-logical, rational, insightful, and emotionless. Spoken word, written word and song are all under this element. Swords represent logic, the mind and your thoughts. They deal with problems and troubles, planning, communication, ideas, your intellect and how you use it. Remember that Air is restless, unsettled energy.

Male is the gender given to this suit. Part of that is the penile shape. Another is that the Sword (l'épée), as an instrument of battle, represent enforcement, authority, problem-solving and management. These used to be very gender-biased roles. Many of our common battles now take place on paper. We must use our minds to solve problems.

KEYWORDS:
- Perception
- Decisive
- Analytical
- Intelligence
- Observe
- Hasty
- Rash
- Cold
- Watch
- Anxiety

EXAMPLES:

The Ace of Swords often represents the dawn of a new way of thinking
The Five of Swords suggests intellectual debate
The Eight of Swords often means being surrounded by many conflicting thoughts.

ASSIGNMENT ONE:
Write a paragraph in your journal about how you feel about air. How does it make you feel?

ASSIGNMENT TWO:
What are some other words you can think of for air? Come up with two positive and two negative.

WANDS

Season: Summer
Direction: South
Zodiac: Aries, Leo, Sagittarius
Element: Fire
Realm: Spirit
Tarot: Wands, Batons, Rods
Playing Card: Clubs
Gender: Masculine

Fire is our next stop. When you think of Fire, S, what pops into your head? Depending on how you were affected by it, it could be a gas stove flame, a camp fire or a forest fire. From the simple light of a candle to the raging roar of a volcano, fire is about passion. When this suit shows up in your character readings, they may have a temper control issue.

The direction associated with fire is South. I place it with Summer as well. Wands, rods, batons, sticks and staves are all Fire suits in the Tarot. Think of things that can serve as fuel. Wands are flammable. This is the suit often swapped with Air but I think it works best in the Wands suit. Wands are the Clubs in the everyday playing deck.

Growth is a key element in this suit. Most of your Wand cards will show green leaves on the staff. This represents the living aspect. This is the other masculine suit. We are talking about life energy here so think sperm and sex and bumping of the uglies. The Rider-Waite Ace of Wands has a definite penis shape to it. When you see a Wand passion and enthusiasm are being brought into play or into question. There is also a sense of speed to this suit.

The Zodiac signs are Aries, Leo and Sagittarius.

Mars and the Sun are two of the planets. This is spirit, energy, illumination. But it is also a destroyer. It burns you up. Wears you out. Explosive and dynamic, this suit is moving. Good or bad, fire is about inspiration, action and creativity. The letter Yod (Primal Energy) is from the Tetragrammaton.

Even when a fire has raged through a forest, there is room for new growth. But remember that fire comes in several levels so it can be a quiet banked blaze as well as a blazing inferno. For your character, you can use Wands in many ways. For careers, consider firefighter or arsonist. They could be a lobbyist or spiritual leader.

Fire, like all the elements has both good and bad inherent. You can't cook a decent steak without a flame, but you can also burn Chicago down if you aren't careful. A lot of fire showing in a story arc always makes me think of a passionately lived life like that of Frida Kahlo or Beverly Sills. How does fire make you feel? It's important to take your own slant into consideration when working with the Tarot--especially as a writer. You want to bring your voice into the story. It's really the only reason to tell a story to me. Others can see things how I see them if only for a few hundred pages at a time.

KEYWORDS:
    Inspire
    Create
    Passion
    Invigorating
    Explosive
    Destroy
    Erupt

Consuming
Burn

What are some other key words you can find?

EXAMPLES:

The Ace of Wands suggests an enthusiastic beginning to a new project
The Five of Wands represents lively, good-natured but intense competition
The Eight of Wands can mean rapid changes and advancement of a project

ASSIGNMENT ONE:
Write a paragraph in your journal about how you feel about fire. How does it make you feel?

ASSIGNMENT TWO:
What are some other words you can think of for fire? Come up with two positive and two negative.

CUPS
  Season: Autumn
  Direction: West
  Zodiac: Cancer, Scorpio, Pisces
  Element: Water
  Realm: Heart
  Tarot: Cups, Chalices, Bowls
  Playing Card: Hearts
  Gender: Feminine

"Water, water everywhere and not a drop to drink." Or so said Samuel Coleridge in his Ancient Mariner piece. This is our third suit of the Tarot. It is the heart of the Tarot for me because of its association with emotions. That also may be because as a Pisces with a Scorpio moon, I am an emotional reader.

Consider that water is love and the cup is the human soul. Each card represents some lesson or challenge on how to best fill that cup with love. This is a feminine suit that deals with relationship and all aspects of emotional life. It carries a meaning of appreciation of beauty.

Water is mutable but it is not a weak element. A steady drip can wear a hole in the densest of rocks. The three signs of the Zodiac for water are Cancer, Scorpio and Pisces. NOTE: Not Aquarius. It is a common misconception that Aquarius, the water bearer, is a water sign.

This is a pretty familiar suit in movies and books. Cups are about love after all. But you have to remember that it is for all emotions so even anger can come into play here. Anger is a passionate emotion so that lives here and in the Fire suit as well. Big emotions as well as small are represented by cups. You have heartbreak and new love as well as all of those things that deal with how we communicate with the people around us. This is more personal communication whereas Swords are more logic-based.

Now investigate the other things such as addiction (particularly alcoholism) that Cups represent. Overindulging in things that are bad (or good) for you are under this suit. An internet addiction might show as cups and swords reversed. Creative pursuits require an emotional component which is why this is the suit of the tortured artistic soul. A poet may have cups and swords in their lives. This is also a suit for intuitive powers such as gut hunches, mother's instinct and intuition.

Visions, poems, music and love all come into play here. A very famous cup is often associated with this Suit--the Holy Grail. If you are not familiar with the travails of the Knights of the Round Table, you might want to research that. Each one who set out on the quest for the Holy Grail was affected in one way or another. Some lost their lives while others their minds.

Another cup image is the womb. Filled with fluid, it was the first home all of us knew. Water, for this reason, can represent maternal feelings. So you can layer in that this suit holds memories and the idea of sacredness as well as motherhood. And so many liquids can be used here. Whiskey as the water of life. Blood as well. For your characters you might view Cups as things that they can empty or fill up. Sometimes they just need to drink more deeply to access something they think is missing.

KEYWORDS:
- Soothing
- Calm
- Fluid
- Dreams
- Intuition
- Limiting
- Overwhelming
- Depressive
- Obsession
- Co-dependent

EXAMPLES:

The Ace of Cups suggests an awakening interest
The Five of Cups suggests a loss with mixed feelings
The Eight of Cups can mean walking away from emotions that have been outgrown

ASSIGNMENT ONE:
Write a paragraph in your journal about how you feel about water. How does it make you feel?

ASSIGNMENT TWO:
What are some other words you can think of for water? Come up with two positive and two negative.

PENTACLES
    Season: Winter
    Direction: North
    Zodiac: Taurus, Virgo, Capricorn
    Element: Earth
    Realm: Body
    Tarot: Pentacles, Discs, Stones
    Playing Cards: Diamonds
    Gender: Feminine

Earth, our final frontier. No wait. That isn't quite right.
Or is it? Earth is so vast. It is literally what we stand on. What our homes are built on. Where our loved ones are buried. Earth in the Tarot is represented by pentacles,

coins, stones, rocks, crystals, caves and mountains. Courage, steadfastness, stubbornness, dogmatic—these are all words that can be associated with Earth energy. It represents what has become manifest in the physical world. Some teach you that you can't get to this material, tangible piece without the previous three and that is why Pentacles are traditionally last in the Tarot.

North is the direction I use for Earth. This is a contested point in some arenas where Air is associated with the North because of the coldness. But for me, North is the correct direction for Earth. You are welcome to adjust your associations as you like.

Astrologically speaking, the Earth signs are Taurus, Virgo and Capricorn. Earth is seen as Feminine and hard to move. This element is associated with physical labor, hand crafts, jobs, building and even luck. Mother Nature, your environment--both inside and out--and physical beauty like artwork, sculptures, etc. are all governed by this suit.

Consider that this is about the physical body, health, genetic heritage even. This is how one values oneself and the material things in the world. It's easy to get focused on the money aspect of coins, but this is so much more. It is their community and their family and friends. It is what holds value for this character in their world both Ordinary and after they cross the Threshold. That can be their great-grandmothers antiques or the brand-new VW Bug in their driveway as well as money in the bank. It can also be a marker of their desires for themselves.

When you get this for a character, ask yourself how they fit into their community. Earth is also the most physical of all the suits so you may see hints of what they look like or what they do for a living here. Don't limit yourself to banker as a job. Spread out and see them as a venture capitalist or a potter--both are hands on in different ways.

KEYWORDS:
    Stability
    Bounty
    Generosity
    Responsibility
    Determination
    Staid
    Material loss
    Low self-esteem
    Stubbornness
    Intractability

EXAMPLES:

Ace of Earth represents a new business or seed money.

Five of Earth represents the loss of a home or potential loss.

Eight of Earth represents learning or teaching a skill.

ASSIGNMENT ONE:
Write a paragraph in your journal about how you feel about earth. How does it make you feel?

ASSIGNMENT TWO:
What are some other words you can think of for earth? Come up with two positive and two negative.

Chapter Twenty

Writers Spreads

The reason most people pick up the Tarot cards is to gain insight. To ask a question and get an answer seems easy until you pick that deck up for the first time and discover the awful truth.

There are 78 of the little buggers and every one of them has at least two meanings. Then you have to learn all the symbols. Don't forget the astrological meanings and the Kabbalah as well. Is it any wonder that most people's eyes glaze over as they slowly drop the cards into a heap to collect dust?

This is one of the reasons Tarot consultants use spreads. A spread refers to the way the cards are laid out. Some readers don't use them at all but many do. I find that for those who are not familiar with Tarot that spreads are a great tool.

A spread has positions. Each of these positions have a concept or meaning attached to them. This offers direction to the card that is placed in that spot. For instance, the Queen of Swords can have different interpretations depending on what spot she falls in.

Let's say she falls into the Personality spot of

your Character Cocktail spread. This could mean that her personality is that of an inquisitive, sharp-minded woman who can be overly analytical. However if it falls in the Quirk position of that same spread, it could mean that she has a passion for word puzzles and is a WordsWithFriends™ addict. Oh wait. That's me. Of course, it's common to have bits and pieces of ourselves turn up in our characters.

Here are some of my favorite spreads that I use when creating characters and plotting my books. I encourage you to try them for yourself. Always remember that you are the one in charge. As the writer, if something doesn't sit well with you, change it. Tweak it. It can be fun to take a seemingly impossible character quirk (a bartender who is a recovering addict?) and then turn it into a believable, sympathetic character flaw (Sam Malone from Cheers!)

There are a lot of spreads out there. For the most part, I will be sharing only ones that I have personally created. I will start, though, with the most common spread which is the Celtic Cross. By the way? That's no more Celtic in origin than spaghetti. It is identified with the Golden Dawn from the turn of the twentieth century. The first published reference is from A.E. Waite's The Pictorial Key to the Tarot (1910.) There are ten cards in this layout. You can do this for your hero if you like. Assume he has gone to a psychic to determine what his fate might be.

NOTE: The way I read the Celtic Cross differs from other readers. It is a spread that has seen a lot of tweaks and changes over the years.

CELTIC CROSS SPREAD

Situation now: This represents the immediate issue at hand. It is something on the hero's mind or happening in the here and now. It is most often why the querent, person asking the question, has initiated the reading. It's now.

Influences: Sometimes called "prevailing winds", this position offers up what is happening around the situation. This can be people, attitudes, bank accounts etc. It is what is pushing the situation. This can be good or bad.

Deep past: Here is a spot that has a lot of flexibility in terms of time. For me, I tend to see this as anywhere from 18 months to 3 years back. Rarely is it more recent than that. This shows something or someone that still has influence on the present situation. In this reading, all the cards revolve around the Situation Now card.

Recent past: Generally anywhere from six months to the day before, this card shows something that has occurred that has brought the current situation to a head.

Goal: This card sits above the Situation Now. I see this as a goal that the querent can reach if they stretch. I remind them that they must extend themselves to get this. It's not easy but it is within reach. Sometimes this goal is not one they have even voiced to themselves as attainable.

Near future: As it says, this is the card of the near future. My caveat here is that this can change depending choices made by the querent. So if you see the Chariot Reversed (which can indicate a car accident or car problems), by being hyper vigilant, you can avoid that thus "changing your future."

How others see the querent: Here is an interesting card. When I am reading for my clients, I ask them if they are sure they want to see this card. This is a card of mirrors because it reflects what friends and family see. Note that this is often a card to help the querent see their value rather than their flaws.

Querent's hopes or fears: I've often seen this card be both a hope and a fear. It holds the potential of being a great joy or a deep sorrow. Consider your querent is your heroine who wants to have a family. The Empress (pregnant and abundant) shows up. Her fear could be that she will never be this woman as much as her hope could be that she will be this woman.

Hurdle: Here is a card I've renamed. More commonly called the Block or the Obstacle, this is something your hero must negotiate to achieve the outcome. I call it a hurdle because you can go over, under or around a hurdle, but you can't go through it. You must negotiate it.

Outcome: Here is the final piece of this spread. It is the answer or next step for the present situation. It is what the hero can expect if the Hurdle is overcome. If you want to use this spread as a plot device.

Now let's move into some spreads that I have developed specifically for use with plotting and character creation.

COCKTAIL SPREAD

Next let's examine a spread I do for my characters to deepen them. Often our characters are sketchy at first. We might know one or two things about them like caped crusader who fights crime. But we need more. We need to know what makes them stand out at the League of Justice company picnics. When this happens, I pretend I'm going to a cocktail party with my hero as my guest. Cocktail parties are designed to be free-flowing and you need a quick introduction. For those in the writing business, you can think of this as your Elevator Pitch only for your character. You will draw three cards. The first card is what your character does for a living. The next is why your character does that for a living. And the last card is a personality quirk.

1
2
3

Your Character's Job
Your Character's Personality
A Quirk

For me, the most important card here is the quirk. Let's say your hero's job is saving Metropolis from criminals (Knight of Swords). His personality is the strong, silent type (Emperor). But his quirk? His quirk is that he has this thing for a woman but she doesn't know about his secret identity (Page of Pentacles.) I'm most interested in what makes him unusual, aren't you?

While the cocktail spread gives you a quick look at your character, sometimes you need to go deeper. You as the writer need to know why your character does what he does. Please remember that it will bore the snot out of your reader if you tell them everything you know about your character. This spread is for you. Dribble in this information. Not all of the following questions will apply to all characters so use the ones you like.

Let's imagine that you have hired a company to do a thorough background check on your character. You want to know everything, right? Of course, this spread isn't what a normal background check would ask, but who ever said writers were normal?

BACKGROUND CHECK SPREAD

Mother: What was my hero's relationship with his mother?

Father: What was my hero's relationship with his father?

Childhood: What was the main theme of my hero's childhood?

Best Friend: Who was your hero's best friend? Are they still in the picture?

First Love: What was my hero's relationship with his first love? How did it end is another way to read this position.

Criminal Record: Does my hero have a record? If a card shows up here to indicate he did have a record, you might add two more cards for "What Was the Crime" and "Why Did He Do It?"

College: Did he go? Did he graduate if he did go? Maybe this will show you what he studied.

Current Job: What puts money in the bank for your hero?

Biggest Secret: Shhh, this is what he doesn't want

others to know. It could be simple like a big homicide cop doesn't want anyone knowing he raises begonias or more complex like the woman who used to be a man.

HE SAID/SHE SAID SPREAD

Here's a shocker. Your hero may not always be telling the whole story. If you've ever mediated an argument, you know that there are always three sides. There are the two participants' recounts of what happened. But any good cop (or marriage counselor) will tell you, there's still the middle. The middle is the interesting part because that's generally closer to the real heart of the matter. This spread gives you a way to use Tarot to create and interpret a potential conflict for your hero.

Normally this is my He Said/She Said Spread which I do use in Tarot consultations. For the purposes of this book and your writing, we will change this to Hero Said/Other Person Said. Sadly, that's not as catchy as He Said/She Said so you will have to work with me on this one. The other person could be the heroine (or same-sex romantic partner). But don't rule out doing this for the villain. This gives your villain depth as well. Consider the fact that he or she has feelings and may just feel that they are severely misunderstood. Some even feel passionately that they are on the side of right. Not all villains are evil psychopaths. Some are sincerely misguided megalomaniacs.

I have two versions. One is the short version that uses three cards.

HERO SAID/OTHER PERSON SAID

What the Hero believes
What the other person believes
What the truth of the matter is.

Here is the expanded version that asks the all-important question "Why?" to go further into the heads of the participants.

You can expand this spread by adding in a third person but that can begin to muddy the waters. I recommend sticking with just the two characters.

HERO SAID/OTHER PERSON SAID EXPANDED

What the Hero believes
Why the Hero believes this.
What the other person believes
Why the other person believes this.
What the truth of the matter is.
How can this issue be resolved?

A fun spread is the Lois Lane spread. Most of us instantly know the intrepid reporter love interest of Superman. It was hard for him to dodge her curiosity both as Clark Kent and as Superman. This spread is good for digging into scenes that aren't working. You can figure out what needs to be most urgent and what is working to move the scene forward. If a scene isn't moving the story forward, you need to fix it or forget it.

LOIS LANE SPREAD

WHO answers the question of center stage. Who is important in this scene?

WHAT answers the question of urgency. What is the important action in this scene?

WHEN answers the question of timing. When is this scene taking place?

HOW answers the question of movement. How does this scene move the story forward?

WHY answers the question of motivation. Why is the character doing this?

This is laid out left to right in a straight line.

You can also use this to build your scenes. Something to consider in any scene is how many senses have you used. You always want to have two to three of the five major senses represented. You might imagine that you are a reporter if you are not writing in first person. Don't tell your reader it is hot. Tell them the character's neck had sweat trickling down or that their mouth is so dry they would sell their mother's pearls for a drink. Make your reader reach for their own glass as they read your words.

HERO'S JOURNEY SPREAD

Here are the thirteen steps to my Hero's Journey Spread for your reference. I won't go over what the positions since you already have that in the preceding lessons. The layout is an arch with the last card in the center. The shape of this spread isn't as important as some. If you do vision boards for your writing, you could put the cards up in the original order. Then you might move them around to see how that affects your story. Remember that the Hero's Journey steps don't have to be in the exact order.

Ordinary World
Call to Adventure
Refusal of the Call
Meeting with the Mentor
Crossing First Threshold
Tests, Allies & Enemies
Approach to Inmost Cave
The Ordeal
Reward (Seizing the Sword)
Road Back
Resurrection
Return with Elixir
Theme

One thing to avoid is pulling cards until you get the answer you want. If you are going to use this as a tool, then let the tool have some time to work. Here is a deceptively simple one card method. I use this when I'm stuck on a scene and can't move forward. I pull one card focusing on this question. "What happens right now?" This is a variant on the question so many of my clients ask. "What does the Universe want me to know right now?" Using the phrasing "right now" opens it up while encouraging urgency as well.

There are many other ways to do one card readings. I am a firm believer in open-ended questions rather than yes/no. "What does my hero to know about the relationship struggle he's facing" gives you more information than "Does she love him."

Here are open-ended questions you can ask for your character (or for yourself):

Work

How will my hero's life change if he accepts this job?

How can my hero achieve balance between work and home?

Family

How can my hero keep his relationship with (name) strong and healthy?

How can my hero improve communication with (name)?

How does my hero help (name) through (problem)?

Love

What will make my hero accept love in his life?

What holds my hero back from accepting love?

Money

What is my hero's biggest problem with money?

How does my hero view the role of money in his life?

If you aren't sure of what question to ask, you can separate the twenty-two Major Arcana out of the deck. Shuffle those and pull one. Then reshuffle the entire deck including the card you pulled. Focus on the corresponding question below then cut the deck. The card you pull is the answer to the question.

MAJOR ARCANA QUESTIONS

(0) Fool: What is my hero risking?
(I) Magician: How can my hero use the tools he has now?
(II) High Priestess: What hidden knowledge would help my hero?
(III) Empress: How will my hero create in this situation?
(IV) Emperor: What decision does my hero need to stand firm on?
(V) Hierophant: What rules can my hero use to his advantage?
(VI) Lovers: Who can my hero trust?
(VII) Chariot: In what way can my hero take charge of his own journey?
(VIII) Strength: How can my hero tap into their power to face the challenges ahead?
(IX) Hermit: How can my hero learn more about this situation?
(X) The Wheel: What unknown opportunity could be a game-changer for my hero?
(XI) Justice: What legal issues is my hero unaware of? What laws could be broken?
(XII) Hanged Man: When can letting go of control do for my hero in this situation?
(XIII) Death: What does my hero need to let go of in order to make progress?
(XIV) Temperance: Where does my hero need to practice more moderation?
(XV) Devil: Who or what tempts my hero to do the wrong thing?
(XVI) Tower: What in my hero's life could fall apart now?

(XVII) Star: What is my hero's true goal?
(XVIII) Moon: What influences are affecting my hero? How can my hero find his way through the confusion?
(XIX) Sun: What new things do I need to prepare for?
(XX) Judgment: How can my hero shed his old fears?
(XXI) World: What is the biggest thing that can happen in this situation?

EXAMPLES:

Using the question for Death, I pulled the Five of Cups. So the answer to "what does my hero need to let go of in order to make progress" could be that he must let go of regret. This opened me up to wonder what he was regretting. If I still had a question, I would have asked, "Who or what does my hero regret the most?"

Chapter Twenty One
The End

Final Thoughts

As Carol Burnett says, "I'm so glad we've had this time together." I hope you have enjoyed it as well. By working through all of the lessons, you will have completed--if not the book--a well fleshed-out story arc. You now have more tools for your writer's toolbox.

As Hemingway so earnestly says, it's the journey that matters. You can take this journey for any future projects as well. It's in your toolbox now.

I'd love to hear from you about your journey as well. Your testimonial, blog review, thoughts--all are welcome. What worked for you? How did your story emerge for you? Let me know.

Here are a few other books (Tarot and writing both) that I recommend:

- Rachel Pollack's Tarot Wisdom: Spiritual Teachings and Deeper Meanings
- Mary K. Greer's 21 Ways to Read a Tarot Card

- Tarot for Life: Reading the Cards for Everyday Guidance and Growth
- GMC: Goal, Motivation, and Conflict
- Writing Down the Bones: Freeing the Writer Within (Shambhala Library)
- Eats, Shoots & Leaves: The Zero Tolerance Approach to Punctuation

Above all else, to thine own voice be true. It's always been about your voice, your style, your story. Don't let anyone take that away from you. Ever!

CPSIA information can be obtained
at www.ICGtesting.com
Printed in the USA
BVHW071111310121
599198BV00045B/1445